Japu Ji Sahib and Srimad Bhagavad Gita

A Spark of Enlightenment

Dr. H. Prashad

D K's BOOKS FOR ALL

Delhi-110052

First Published 2011

ISBN 13: 978-81-7386-287-8
ISBN 10: 81-7386-287-7

Published By
DK's BOOKS FOR ALL
(an imprint of Low Price Publications)
A-6, Second Floor, Nimri Commercial Centre,
Ashok Vihar Phase-4, Delhi - 110 052
Tel.: +91 11 2730 2453
website: www.Lppindia.com
e-mail: info@Lppindia.com

Printed At
D K Fine Art Press P Ltd.
Delhi-110052

PRINTED IN INDIA

Dedicated To

The Almighty, Cosmic Power, Supernal and Silence Formless Oneness, whose Blessings, Radiance, Continued Inspiration, Booming Energy and Silent Guidance that has graced me to follow the path of Peace and Enlightenment for realizing the Ultimate Truth and Self – Realization and to be always being in Him for ultimate mergence in the Absolute.

July 2010   **Dr. H. Prashad**

Preface

By the inspiration of Almighty and His divine grace, after life long spiritual engrossment the book on "Japu Ji Sahib & Srimad Bhagavad Gita-A Spark of Enlightenment" has been accomplished.

The book deals with explanation of each Pauri of Japuji Sahib in the light of Vedanta philosophy, as has been conceived and perceived by the divine grace. The explanation is unique in many ways since truth is always perfect in multifold dimensions. Followed by explanation in English of each Pauri, the equivalent Slokas/Verses of different Chapters of Srimad Bhagavad Gita, more relevant to the concerned Pauri are written in Sanskrit along with the standard published explanation in English by the reputed authors. The exact equivalent verses of each Pauri could not be allocated. However, complete Japuji Sahib with due explanation, as conceived/experienced by the divine grace, with the relevant verses of Srimad Bhagavat Gita, has been accomplished.

Since from my early age I was highly fascinated by the philosophical contents of Japuji Sahib and the Vedanta philosophy of Srimad Bhagavad Gita, and with time I experienced the divine unison in modes of expressions in these classical wonders that has lead to precipitate and concise my thoughts in the form of this book, which I humbly consider the natural showers of His grace on the pattern of present contemplation. This divine light appeared after going through the commentaries of different reputed authors of JapuJi Sahib and Srimad Bhagavad Gita. Almighty alone is the force behind expressions and expanse in all modes of His own glory.

As I understand, no book in this particular pattern has appeared so far. I feel this book will be an integration of spiritual one-ness since source and origin of the mysterious divine knowledge is the same by the one-ness of divinity.

In the light of the above, I would like to express to the spiritual aspirants that there is no end to conceive the depth of each word of these mysterious classics, and one can visualize that by any angle at any depth, the expressions and ideology will be perfect in all modes.

Finally, I would like to express my gratitude to the Cosmic Power, the Almighty, who has infused me to take up this divine accomplishment and boomed me with the source of untiring and inexhaustible energy by His Blessings, Radiance, Continued Inspiration and Silence Guidance to nurture me all the time to follow and pursue the mysterious divine path to be with the Self and Self-alone. Also, I acknowledge the silent participation of my wife, Darshan, son & daughter-in-law Poojan & Gauri, and daughter & son-in-law Shweta & Rajeev with little Kriya and loving Nimay to assist me to climb the ladder of divinity.

Hyderabad   **Dr. H. Prashad**
July 2010

1-2-319/ A, Gagan Mahal
Domal Guda, 302 Central View,
Hyderabad-500029 (India)
Phone: 040-27634907, 09652013280
E-mail:har.prashad@gmail.com

About the Author

Dr. Har Prashad is presently consultant of Centre for Tribology Incorporated, (CETR) USA. He is retired Senior Deputy General Manager (Tribology) from the Bharat Heavy Electricals Limited, Corporate Research and Development Division, Hyderabad. He obtained an M.E. (Hons) degree in Mechanical Engineering in 1970, and subsequently, Ph.D. in Tribology. He worked with the Indian Institute of Petroleum, Dehra Dun, and with the Design Bureau at Bokaro Steel Ltd., Dahnbad, Bihar, before joining BHEL in 1974.

Dr. Prashad has published more than 125 papers in both national and international journals. He is the author of three technical books. The book on "Tribology in Electrical Environments" is published from United Kingdom by Elsevier Publishers in December 2005. The second book on 'Solving Tribology Problems of Rotating Machines " is published by Wood head Publishers, U.K, in February 2006. The third book on "Integral Approaches to Tribo-testing in Mechanical Engineering" is published by CRC,USA in August 2009.

For his achievements, author's name has been included in Marquis Who's Who in the world published in 2001 from USA. Also, his name is included in International Directory of Distinguished Leadership-2001, published by American Biographical Institute. His bio-data is published in the directory of "Contemporary Who's Who -2004" by the same institute.

Furthermore, for his distinguished achievements, Tribology Society of India graced him with Life Time Achievement Award 2010 (Industrial Category) in the Seventh International Conference on Industrial Tribology-2010, held at Ranchi (Organized by Sail Authority of India under the Aegis of Tribology Society of India) on 4th December, 2010.

Besides the above technical books, the book of spiritual sciences on "Solutions of Problems & Remedies of Human Life—A Path of Peace and Enlightenment" is published in August 2010 by DK's Books for All, New Delhi and is being marketed.

Besides being the author of this present book on " Japu Ji Sahib and Shrimad Bhagavad-Gita – A Spark of Enlightenment", he has written another spiritual book to satisfy his spiritual contentment for the benefit of spiritual aspirants and society based on the his pure individual experiences. The book is: " Queries of a Spiritual Aspirant / Sadhaka - in - the Path of Self- Realization". Besides this, he is pursuing other mysterious works in spiritual divine science including "Spikes of Silence by Silence and in Silence" and "Principles of Creative Problem Solving---jewels of Life "by the Wish of Almighty.

Contents

Japuji Sahib

Mulmantra - The Prologue

Ik Onkar

Sat Naam

Karta Purakh

Nirbhau

Nirvair

Akal Murat

Ajuni

*Saibham**

Gurprasad

* pronounced *saibhang* in Punjabi

Explanation

This is the prologue/preface of the Japuji Sahib. *"ik Onkar"* by itself is the core, the source. Guru Nanak Ji categorically uses the integer "1", one, "ik", indicating one Supreme Cosmic Power / Light, and all is derived from this "One" governing infinite force, the Almighty, the Infinite, who is above generator, preserver and destroyer i.e. Brahma, Vishnu and Mahesh.

It establishes an undisputed and complete "Oneness" of the Almighty. Subsequent words in the prologue further expand this concept.

Satnam signifies that Truth alone is God. Also, Sat is the micro/nano "Essence", and it is the essential divine force for His existence.

Karta Purakh further affirms God as the sole doer, the creator.

Nirbhau is used to explain that God is sans fear. By using *Nirbhau* Guru Nanak Ji is establishing the Absolute nature or Supremeness of God. Truth is uttered by the one, who is sans fear. A fearful person cannot speak the truth.

Nirvair is used to explain that God is sans enmity. God is the one, who judges and also punishes. One is the sole creator, is Absolute that pervades in total creation. Thus *Nirvair* affirms God's Supremacy.

Akal Murat professes God to be eternal, beyond time, changeless and ever fresh and new. .

Ajuni professes God to be unborn and not mutable. God is immutable.

Saibham explains God as self-effulgent and Supreme.

Gurprasad is explained as the blessing through an Enlightened/Self realized master. Enlightenment is His Divine Grace. Thus, Guru Nanak Ji uses *Gurprasad* to conclusively proclaim that the "One" God, the Almighty can be realized only with His divine grace and Almighty power. God's realization is His blessings and not just by the individual's self-efforts.

In brief then, the prologue or the Mulmantra in the Japu ji Sahib, is the foundation of the Philosophy of Shri Guru Granth Sahib that affirms the existence of "One" God, the Almighty, pervading the Cosmos and yet staying independent of it. Rest of the Japu ji Sahib is an exposition of the Mulmantra, while Shri Guru Granth Sahib as an exposition of the Japu ji itself.

The Mulmantra also embodies itself in the form of an invocation and affirmation of human faith in the existence of a Supreme reality identified as Truth. By simply saying "*ik* Onkar", one invokes the Supreme and seeks His grace, so that one may lead a truthful life, fearlessly and with compassion to all.

In the nutshell, Mulmantra depicts that Almighty as only One Cosmic Light that governs generation, preservation and dissolution, and exists truly without any definite shape and size. It is changeless, beyond the perception of human senses. It is true existence in all the creations and it is as an essence in the micro/nano form of/in the natural growth by the divine force. Without this true existence of Cosmic Light, the Almighty, creation cannot exist. This omnipresent Cosmic Light is the Creator of the Universe and It is consequently without any fear and enmity to His own creation. This Universal Cosmic Light nourishes His own manifestation with Cosmic love and affinity with Its Own Cosmic laws. The Almighty/Supreme Cosmic Light not appeared from Yoni, so It's existence is beyond time, and it is always new and fresh. This cosmic illumination is eternal, Self created by Cosmic means. It is unborn so it is beyond death, however It can materialize in any shape by His own Will, which is beyond limitation of time, space and causation.

This Cosmic Light/Almighty is Self –effulgent and beyond laws of creation. This Cosmic light is/can be experienced by the mercy of the Almighty/Cosmic Light alone as the divine blessings. The presence of divine light in Creation can merge in this Cosmic Light, the Absolute, as a beam of divine light and It is only possible by the blessings and Will of source Cosmic Light./ the Almighty/ the Absolute.

Japu

(*sloka*)

> *Aad Sach*
>
> *Jugad Sach*
>
> *Hai Bhi Sach*
>
> *Nanak Hosi Bhi Sach*

True before creation

True through all ages

True also today

says Nanak,

True He shall eternally be.

Explanation

This (*sloka*) *Japu* further reaffirms the Supremacy of God. And briefly *reiterates* the same as in the prologue.

The presence of the divine Cosmic Light is true from time memorial and Its existence is from generations, and It is beyond time. Even in the present time Cosmic Light presence is beyond question, and truth of Its existence is continued as it was. Guru Nanak Ji merged in that Cosmic Light and revealed this universal truth forever to the human race, which is unquestioned.

Equivalent Verses of Srimad Bhagavad Gita

(Mulmantra and Japu)

Chapter 10

An Account of God's Glory

The Iinfinite Manifestation of the Unmanifest Spirit

The Unborn and Beginningless, Beyond Form and Conception (Verses 2-3)

न मे विदुः सुरगणाः प्रभवं न महर्षयः।
अहमादिर्हि देवानां महर्षीणां च सर्वशः ॥२॥

2. "Neither gods nor great sages know my origin, for I am the primal Source from which all of them have arisen."

यो मामजमनादिं च वेत्ति लोकमहेश्वरम्।
असम्मूढः स मर्त्येषु सर्वपापैः प्रमुच्यते ॥३॥

3. "The wise man among mortals, who knows my reality as the birthless, eternal, and supreme God of the entire world, is freed from all sins."

The Diverse Modifications of God's Nature (Verses 4-6)

बुद्धिर्ज्ञानमसम्मोहः क्षमा सत्यं दमः शमः।
सुखं दुःखं भवोऽभावो भयं चाभयमेव च ॥४॥
अहिंसा समता तुष्टिस्तपो दानं यशोऽयशः।
भवन्ति भावा भूतानां मत्त एव पृथग्विधाः ॥५॥

4-5. "All the manifold qualities with which beings are endowed: will, knowledge, freedom from delusion, forgiveness, truth, restraint of Senses and mind, happiness and unhappiness, creation and destruction, fear and fearlessness, as well as abstinence from the desire to harm, equanimity of mind, contentment, penance, charity, fame, and ignominy-are provided by none but me."

महर्षयः सप्त पूर्वे चत्वारो मनवस्तथा ।
मद्भावा मानसा जाता येषां लोक इमाः प्रजाः ॥६॥

6. "The seven great sages, the four who had been earlier than them, as well as Manu and others from whom all mankind has sprung, have all been shaped by the operation of my will."

In Joy and Devotion, the Wise Adore Him (Verses 7-11)

एतां विभूतिं योगं च मम यो वेत्ति तत्त्वतः ।
सोऽविकम्पेन योगेन युज्यते नात्र संशयः ॥७॥

7. "The one who knows the reality of my exalted magnificence and the might of my yog doubtless partakes of my nature by becoming one with me through meditation."

अहं सर्वस्य प्रभवो मत्तः सर्वं प्रवर्तते ।
इति मत्वा भजन्ते मां बुधा भावसमन्विताः ॥८॥

8. "Aware of the reality that I am the source of all creation as also the motive that stirs it to effort, and possessed of faith and devotion, wise men remember and worship only me."

मच्चित्ता मद्गतप्राणा बोधयन्तः परस्परम्।
कथयन्तश्च मां नित्यं तुष्यन्ति च रमन्ति च।।९।।

9. "They who anchor their minds on me, sacrifice their breath to me, and are contented with speaking only of my greatness among themselves, always dwell in me."

तेषां सततयुक्तानां भजतां प्रीतिपूर्वकम्।
ददामि बुद्धियोगं तं येन मामुपयान्ति ते।।१०।।

10. "I bestow upon the devotees, who always remember me and adore me with love, that discipline of yog by learning which they attain to none but me."

तेषामेवानुकम्पार्थमहमज्ञानजं तमः।
नाशयाम्यात्मभावस्थो ज्ञानदीपेन भास्वता।।११।।

11. "To extend my grace to them, I dwell in their innermost being and dispel the gloom of ignorance by the radiance of knowledge."

Pauri -1

Explanation

Thinking million times about supreme Cosmic light, maintaining physical purity, pure thoughts, words and deeds and even maintaining all these qualities as a way of proper living for a long duration do not take a human being to the door step of Supreme Cosmic Light, the Almighty. On the other hand thinking about this supreme Cosmic light creates bundle of thoughts in a human mind that diminishes peace of mind, creates turmoil in mind, which take him further away from the Almighty. Absconding talking/minimum talk, by not interacting with any body and by making the physical body still like rock, and maintaining absolute silence to the maximum possible extend, and even becoming one with the silence as if becoming breathless, and even to get merged completely in all these processes, one is still unable to experience the glimpses of divine Cosmic Light/Almighty.

Furthermore loading the self with external divine rituals does not quench the thirst for divine Cosmic Light, and still one is deprived of His grace. As a hungry person can never overcome his hunger without the consumption of food. Keeping bulk food externally on his stomach never fulfills his hunger. In other words desires are not satisfied to be under the influence of desires. Inaddition, if some one is mentally hungry then only food of thoughts can satisfy him and not the gross food. One needs to understand in depth what he basically needs to be/get contented, and have conscious needful boundaries for the same. Various types of intellectual/mental ways or processes adopted very seriously and sincerely for the divine self – realization, does not help at all to get any success in the path of God realization.

To merge in the absolute truth is to avoid hindrances/walls of all untruth and false ways/processes in thoughts, words and deeds, and to be truthful is the only purest/sure and easiest way to climb this ladder of self- realization. But how a humble human being can adopt this tedious path in life?

Guru Nanak Ji says that one must follow the divine laws in all walks of life in eating, living, behaving, interacting with fellow being and seniors/superiors and maintaining strict daily discipline/schedule through out life i.e. Yama and Niyama, besides being always with the Supreme Cosmic Light on the mental plane. Thus, on one side it seems to be the easiest path, but on other side it is the most difficult path since in proper living one need to live above the attraction of senses and greedy earthy desires. But, Guru Nank in Japu Ji depicts this path as the easiest path in the present time of Kali Yuga.

Here, saying of Guru Nanak Ji can also be understood in this way that one must feel contented under all conditions that the Lord has provided him. He must treat happiness and distress equally considering these all are by the Wish of Almighty, and one has no role to play except to accept happily what He is pouring, as His blessings. One must be completely surrendered to His Will. Surrender to His Will and having no desires of his own make a person truly religious and devoted and this allows him to be with the Almighty.

Equivalent Verses of Srimad Bhagavad Gita (Pauri 1)

Chapter 18

In Truth Do I Promise Thee: Thou Shalt Aattain Me

Summary of the Gita's Message: How God-Realization is Attained (Verses 50-53)

सिद्धिं प्राप्तो यथा ब्रह्म तथाप्नोति निबोध मे।
समासेनैव कौन्तेय निष्ठा ज्ञानस्य या परा।।५०।।

50. "Learn in brief from me, O son of Kunti, of how one who is immaculate achieves realization of the Supreme Being, which represents the culmination of knowledge."

बुद्ध्या विशुद्धया युक्ते धृत्यात्मानं नियम्य च।
शब्दादीन्विषयांस्त्यक्त्वा रागद्वेषौ व्युदस्य च।।५१।।

51. "Blessed with a pure intellect, firmly in command of the Self, with objects of sensual gratification like sound forsaken, with both fondness and revulsion destroyed,-"

विविक्तसेवी लघ्वाशी यतवाक्कायमानसः।
ध्यानयोगपरो नित्यं वैराग्यं समुपाश्रितः।।५२।।

52. "Dwelling in seclusion, eating frugally, subdued in mind, speech and body, incessantly given to the yog of meditation, firmly resigned,-"

अहङ्कारं बलं दर्पं कामं क्रोधं परिग्रहम्।
विमुच्य निर्ममः शान्तो ब्रह्मभूयाय कल्पते।।५३।।

53. "Giving up conceit, arrogance of power, yearning, ill humour, and acquisitiveness, devoid of attachment, and in possession of a mind at repose, a man is worthy of becoming one with God."

Pauri - 2

Hukami Hovan Aakar Hukam Na Kahiya Jai

Hukami Hovan Jiv Hukam Mile Vadiyai

Hukami Uttam Nich Hukam Likhe Dukh Sukh Paiyeh

Ikna Hukami Bakshish Ik Hukami Sada Bhuvaiyeh

Hukme Andar Sabh Ko Bahar Hukam Na Koi

Nanak Hukame Je Bujhe Te Haumae Kahe Na Koi

Explanation

His /Cosmic Supreme Light inexpressible will creates all forms and all creatures. Life breeds and progresses by His will, whether Highs and lows; or in different grades.

Joys and sorrows experienced by creatures are as per His Will. His/Cosmic divine light, Will, gives deliverance/ blessings to some; while others grope in the cycle of birth and death. Everything is within His order/command, nothing is without the Will of Almighty/Cosmic Light.

Guru Nanak Ji says, understanding His Will annihilates the ego's ills of a human being. He becomes selfless and his life pattern changes gradually as he conceives His Will. Soon by His grace he becomes different personality in this life it self.

In short, Guru Nanak Ji explains that every activity of this universe is by His grace and nothing is beyond His Will. When a human being really understands the depth of the Cosmic drama, his egoism vanishes. He perceives the mysterious command of the Almighty that what is being done by Him/ Cosmic Light, is by the strict divine laws and it is beyond apprehension of a common creature. Basically, what is happening with an individual is by the reactions of his actions in this life or may be of previous lives. Cosmic Light/Almighty is Himself much away/above from all these disparities. He is not involved still every activity is as per His Command.

Equivalent Verses of Srimad Bhagavad Gita (Pauri 2)

Chapter 18

In Truth Do I Promise Thee: Thou Shalt Attain Me

Summary of the Gita's Message: How God-Realization is Attained (Verses 54-55)

ब्रह्मभूतः प्रसन्नात्मा न शोचति न काङ्क्षति ।
समः सर्वेषु भूतेषु मद्भक्तिं लभते पराम् ।।५४।।

54. "In this serene-tempered man, who views all beings equally, who abides intently in the Supreme Being, neither grieving over nor hankering after anything, there is fostered a faith in me that transcends all else."

भक्त्या मामभिजानाति यावान्यश्चास्मि तत्त्वतः ।
ततो मां तत्त्वतो ज्ञात्वा विशते तदनन्तरम् ।।५५।।

55. "Through his transcendental faith he knows my essence well, what my reach is, and having thus known my essence he is at once united with me."

Pauri - 3

Gave Ko Tan Hove Kise Tan

Gave Ko Dat Jane Nisan

Gave Ko Gun Vadiyaian Chaar

Gave Ko Vidiya Vikham Vichaar

Gave Ko Saje Kare Tan Khe

Gave Ko Jiv Lae Phir De

Gave Ko Jape Dise Dur

Gave Ko Vekhe Hadra Hadur

Kathana Kathi Na Aave Tote

Kathi Kathi Kathi Koti Koti Kote

Denda De Lande Thak Pae

Juga Jugantar Khaie Khaye

Hukami Hukam Chalae Rah

Nanak Vigse Beparvah

Explanation

Some sing His Might and got blessed with a type of desired Might by His Blessings. This also means that one sings about

His power based on his own capability. His whole activity revolves around for projection of the power of Almighty.

Some sing about His effulgence by counting their blessings, which God have poured in.

Some praise His uncounted wonderful virtues and greatness.

Some praise Him by their meager understanding for His deep and complex Cosmic knowledge, and His involved manifestation of Divine Light philosophically.

Some praise Him as the mighty force creating and beautifying universe and wonderful physical human body, and later destroy it to merge into the soil.

Some accept Him as His mysterious Leela/drama/play being destroyer and creator.

Some sing since He appears very far away from them, from their mind to get immerge in Him, and understand Him by their wisdom.

Some sing realizing that He is very close and they are in Him by their mind. And their thoughts are always immerged in Him. He is omnipresent.

However, one may say, there is no end to sing about Him./ Supreme Cosmic Light even if one sing virtues of His grace million and million of time. He has infinite virtues. Even infinite is small expression to express His virtues.

He keeps giving us for ages without any pause, and never tired. Only recipients are exhausted taking His grace/blessings.

From time memorial, from ages, creatures are fed by His grace but His treasures are still the same.

His creation continues to enjoy His bounties.

By His Will, and by His Command only He shows the way.

Says Nanak, by His Carefree, happy, unattached nature and divine laws He enjoys and develops His creation. He gives abundance of opportunities to His creation to develop in all respects; He/the Almighty exhibits lot of patience for their development. With all His efforts, He Himself is not bothered and is always carefree/unattached but goes on trying for the development and welfare of His creation with unending patience, His grace and blessings.

This stanza explains the phenomenon of One Cosmic Light manifesting in many different ways. And, Its multitude is shown here expressing His worship in different dimensions/ prospective as conceived by the creatures. It is basically worship of One Cosmic omnipresent supreme light as an individual creature conceives and perceives His blessings. Using the analogy of the many observing the One, there seems to be a reflection upon the various modes of an individual thinking of Almighty grace, expressing the Inexpressible - the Silent One, the Cosmic Light by one's own way and unique prospective.

Equivalent Verses of Srimad Bhagavad Gita (Pauri 3)

Chapter 7

The Nature of Spirit and Spirit of Nature

Perceiving the Spirit Behind the Dream-Shadows of Nature (Verses 28-30)

येषां त्वन्तगतं पापं जनानां पुण्यकर्मणाम् ।
ते द्वन्द्वमोहनिर्मुक्ता भजन्ते मां दृढव्रताः ॥२८॥

28. "But they who worship me in every way are selflessly engaged in good deeds, free from sin and delusion, arising from the conflicts of attachment and repulsion, and of firm intent."

जरामरणमोक्षाय मामाश्रित्य यतन्ति ये ।
ते ब्रह्म तद्विदुः कृत्स्नमध्यात्मं कर्म चाखिलम् ॥२९॥

29. "Only they who strive for liberation from the cycle of birth and death by finding shelter under me succeed in knowing God, spiritual wisdom and all action."

साधिभूताधिदैवं मां साधियज्ञं च ये विदुः ।
प्रयाणकालेऽपि च मां ते विदुर्युक्तचेतसः ॥३०॥

30."They who know me as the presiding Spirit in all beings (adhibhut) and gods (adhidaiv), and in yagya (adhiyagya), and whose minds are fixed on me, know me at the end."

Pauri - 4

Explanation

Supreme true Master/Cosmic Light as is He, the changeless, so His command and laws are changeless, without any ambiguity, is only expressed by the true heartily language of love. This love can be of any kind towards Him, may be of devotee, may be of child for mother or may be the love of a beloved.

The way one seeks and beseeches by his prayers, in the same way the Almighty bestows His blessings.

What should one offer to the Almighty that His Grace is received? Or what way the gratitude must be expressed to Almighty for all His grace and blessings. In other words How should one pray to express that Almighty may merit/bestow

His love? It is very clear that one must speak sweetly with love so that listener develops devotion and love towards the speaker. Guru Nanak emphasis the language of heart in dealings and communication and not merely hollow spoken words from the mouth so as to have strong social life and smooth sailing in relations in all walk of life.

Guru Nanak Ji explains that one must contemplate, chant His divine name and meditate His glory during the holy twilight hour of each morning regularly and religiously to lead a disciplined life.

Blessings of the Almighty gifted us physical body in this human birth so as to enter the divine door to attain liberation in this birth by performing good deeds/actions and devotion towards Him.

Says Nanak, thus one must realize that the One all-in-all is the Truth, which is perfect, fully filled, changeless and omnipresent.

Equivalent Verses of Srimad Bhagavad Gita (Pauri 4)

Chapter 17

Three Kinds of Faith

Aum-Tat-Sat: God the Father, Son, and Holy Ghost (Verses 23-28)

ॐ तत्सदिति निर्देशो ब्रह्मणस्त्रिविधः स्मृतः।
ब्राह्मणास्तेन वेदाश्च यज्ञाश्च विहिताः पुरा।।२३।।

23. "Om, tat , and sat are three epithets used for the
Supreme Being from whom at the outset there came forth
the Brahmin, Ved, and yagya."

तस्मादोमित्युदाहृत्य यज्ञदानतपःक्रियाः।
प्रवर्तन्ते विधानोक्ताः सततं ब्रह्मवादिनाम्।।२४।।

24. "It is hence that the deeds of yagya, charity, and
penance, as ordained by scripture, are always initiated by
the devotees of Ved with a resonant utterance of the
syllable OM."

तदित्यनभिसन्धाय फलं यज्ञतपःक्रियाः ।
दानक्रियाश्च विविधाः क्रियन्ते मोक्षकाङ्क्षिभिः।।२५।।

25. "Stripped of desire for any reward and holding that God
is all pervading, persons who aspire to the ultimate bliss
embark on the tasks of yagya, penance, and charity as
ordained by scripture."

सद्भावे साधुभावे च सदित्येतत्प्रयुज्यते।
प्रशस्ते कर्मणि तथा सच्छब्दः पार्थ युज्यते।।२६।।

26. "Sat is employed to express the ideas of truth and excellence, and, O Parth, the word is also used to denote a propitious act."

यज्ञे तपसि दाने च स्थितिः सदिति चोच्यते।
कर्म चैव तदर्थीयं सदित्येवाभिधीयते।।२७।।

27. "And it is said that the condition inherent in yagya, penance, and charity, as well as the endeavour to attain to God, is also real."

अश्रद्धया हुतं दत्तं तपस्तप्तं कृतं च यत्।
असदित्युच्यते पार्थ न च तत्प्रेत्य नो इह।।२८।।

28. "Therefore, O Parth, is it said that, devoid of faith, the oblation and alms that are offered and the penance that is suffered, as well as all other similar ventures, are all false, for they can do us good neither in this world nor in the next."

Pauri - 5

Thapia Na Jaye Kita Na Hoye

Aape Aap Niranjan Soye

Jin Sevia Tin Payea Maan

Nanak Gaviye Guni Nidhaan

Gaviye Suniye Mun Rakhiye Bhau

Dukh Parhar Sukh Ghar Lai Jaye

Gurmukh Nadam Gurmukh Vedam

Gurmukh Rahia Samai

Gur Isar Gur Gorakh Barma

Gur Parbati Mai

Je Haun Jana Akhan Nahi

Kehna Kathan Na Jayee

Guran Ik Deh Bujhai

Sabna Jiyan Ka Ik Daata

So Mein Visar Na Jayee

Explanation

He cannot be installed nor shaped.

He is the formless One. He is not created, and Maya, the delusion has no role to play with Him. He cannot be created.

He is self created and no evil tendencies can approach Him. He is purest in all respects. He is above all, and nothing is comparable/equivalent to Him.

Those who serve Him i.e. serving the mankind selflessly, and worship Him, they are honored in all walks of life. Also, those who have experienced/realized Him, they are illuminated

Says Nanak, Sing the glories of that great virtuous One, the Supreme Cosmic Light. Sing, praise and listen His divine glories with a heart full of love so that love for Him is permanently installed in the heart by fully understanding the meaning of His words of praise, and heart becomes cheerful with divinity.

By this process of love, when love is installed fully in the heart, shedding of miseries of life is continued, which finally establishes home of all joys in the heart.

The words of Guru are the divine voice. The words of Guru are the preaching/saying of Vedas. All divine knowledge dissolved in supernatural way in the voice of Guru that flows out from the deep meaning of His sayings.

The formless Guru is God/ the supreme Cosmic Light, the One personified as Shiva, Vishnu and Brahma. The Guru, the God can be formless and may be with form. Or, also the mother Goddess *Parbati, as the symbol of power.*

The Almighty position is such as If, at all, I know, I shall not be able to say/describe Him. Since God is beyond words and human perception. Also, if I don't know Him, I cannot describe. However, even if I know, He is beyond description. In other words, the inexpressible cannot be expressed.

My Guru has revealed the riddle that of all creation and for all creation, He is the bestowal. So it is prayed that, this I should never forget in my life since He is compassionate and filled with the feeling of love for the mankind.

Equivalent Verses of Srimad Bhagavad Gita (Pauri 5)

Chapter 18

In Truth Do I Promise Thee: Thou Shalt Attain Me

Summary of the Gita's Message: How God-Realization is Attained (Verses 57-62)

चेतसा सर्वकर्माणि मयि सन्न्यस्य मत्परः।
बुद्धियोगमुपाश्रित्य मच्चित्तः सततं भव।।५७।।

57. "Earnestly resigning all your deeds to me, finding shelter in me, and embracing the yog of knowledge, you should ever fix your mind on me."

मच्चित्तः सर्वदुर्गाणि मत्प्रसादात्तरिष्यसि।
अथ चेत्त्वमहङ्कारान्न श्रोष्यसि विनङ्क्ष्यसि।।५८।।

58. "Ever resting on me, you will be saved from all afflictions and gain deliverance, but you shall be destroyed if out of arrogance you do not pay heed to my words ."

यदहङ्कारमाश्रित्य न योत्स्य इति मन्यसे।
मिथ्यैष व्यवसायस्ते प्रकृतिस्त्वां नियोक्ष्यति।।५९।।

59. "Your egotistic resolve not to fight is surely mistaken, for your nature will compel you to rake up arms in the war."

स्वभावजेन कौन्तेय निबद्धः स्वेन कर्मणा।
कर्तुं नेच्छसि यन्मोहात् करिष्यस्यवशोऽपि तत्।।६०।।

60. "Bound by your natural calling even against your resolve, O son of Kunti, you will have to undertake the deed you are reluctant to do because of your self-deception."

ईश्वर: सर्वभूतानां हृद्देशेऽर्जुन तिष्ठति।
भ्रामयन्सर्वभूतानि यन्त्रारूढानि मायया।।६१।।

61. "Propelling all living things that bestride a body-which is but a contrivance-by his maya, O Arjun, God abides in the hearts of all beings."

तमेव शरणं गच्छ सर्वभावेन भारत।
तत्प्रसादात्परां शान्तिं स्थानं प्राप्स्यसि शाश्वतम्।।६२।।

62. "Seek refuge with all your heart, O Bharat, in that God by whose grace you will attain to repose and the everlasting, ultimate bliss."

Pauri - 6

Explanation

By the Wish and blessings of the Almighty, the Supreme Cosmic Light, one can divert/move his intrinsic energies towards Him, meditate on His name and can immerge in the divine ocean by locating the source of life force/energy in himself and take holy bath in the nectar of life pranic energy as if taking a dip in the holy water of the body temple. It is like going to the places of pilgrimages and taking bath in the divine water of His pure name in such places. Without His blessings, chanting of His name and being one/merge in such chanting, and visiting places of divine worship are not feasible. Furthermore, to have such desires/intentions to spend time, money and efforts for the Almighty are by the His Wish. Of his own one can neither think and nor spend his time for the divine glory either visiting holy places or even to have a thought of His name with love, and locating the source of life energy in himself for getting merge in the divine glory. In short meditation on Him is not possible without His grace.

In this vast world created by Almighty, one experiences, observes and feels gradually that in this mundane life nothing can succeed without His grace and blessings. In any success whether in worldly affairs or in spiritual matters, on one side individual efforts are needed but on the other side without the grace of Almighty, there is absolutely no gain, and all human efforts are in vain. Here the efforts may be understood to be just observer maintaining silence, and leaving every thing in His hands to get His blessings/grace.

If we follow command of Guru/Almighty to execute worldly affairs and to make progress in divine life, this will enhance our wisdom, discrimination and sharpen our intellect as if we are enriched in our physical holdings with pearls, jewels and costliest diamonds of the earth. In other words, we tend to achieve perfection to become perfect like Almighty, and all divine virtues get cultivated in us provided we follow His command to be mentally silent and be one with Him/His name.

I pray to Almighty to bless me and enrich me with wisdom, self-realization and perfect understanding such that I always remember, who cares for the whole creation, and I get merge in His blessings and always have His divine grace.

Equivalent Verses of Srimad Bhagavad Gita (Pauri 6)

Chapter 8

The Imperishable Absolute: Beyond The Cycles Of Creation and Dissolution

The Method of Attaining the Supreme (Verses 12-15)

सर्वद्वाराणि संयम्य मनो हृदि निरुध्य च।
मूर्ध्न्याधायात्मनः प्राणमास्थितो योगधारणाम्।।१२।।

12. "Shutting the doors of all the senses, that is, restraining them from desire for their objects, confining his intellect within the Self, fixing his life-breath within his mind, and absorbed in yog,..."

ओमित्येकाक्षरं ब्रह्म व्याहरन्मामनुस्मरन्।
यः प्रयाति त्यजन्देहं स याति परमां गतिम्।।१३।।

13. "He who departs from the body intoning OM, which is God in word, and remembering me, attains to salvation."

अनन्यचेताः सततं यो मां स्मरति नित्यशः।
तस्याहं सुलभः पार्थ नित्ययुक्तस्य योगिनः।।१४।।

14. "The yogi who is firmly devoted to me, and who constantly remembers me and is absorbed in me, realizes me with ease."

15. "Accomplished sages who have attained to the ultimate state are no longer subject to transient rebirth which is like a house of sorrows."

Pauri - 7

Explanation

The long life extended by various efforts by practices of Pranayama and by various meditation practices, and different other unknown means without the grace of God does not fetch any satisfaction. It is just worthless even if one has a long life even equivalent to that of four Yuga (Sat Yuga to Kali Yuga i.e. billion of years), and even if it becomes ten fold. Even if one is known in the nine continents of the universe with a great number of followers, and even if every body listen to him very eagerly with great respect, it is of no use. Furthermore, even if some one is well known worldwide and have immense respect/honor, but still if Almighty does not recognizes him or if he is not blessed with God's grace and not achieved absolute mental silence by His grace and immerged in it, no body will bother and talk about him any where, in any walk of life now and in future. He will be considered as the most useless and unimportant creature on the earth. Even criminals will find the faults in his affairs , dealings and behavior. Like a mere worm, he would be considered/accused even by a sinner.

Guru Nanak Ji emphasizes that only the grace of Almighty turns an ordinary human being as virtuous and bless him with all capabilities even if he does not deserve any of the virtues. Also to the virtuous person, God blesses with more virtues and make him glorious. There is no other personality existing in this universe, which can execute such a wonderful activity of gifting the unimaginable divine virtues to an insignificant creature. Non other than God/Cosmic power can show such a merit to a worldly creature.

Equivalent Verses of Srimad Bhagavad Gita (Pauri 7)

Chapter 4

The Supreme Science Of Knowing God

The All-Sanctifying Wisdom, Imparted By A True Guru (Verses 34-37)

तद्विद्धि प्रणिपातेन परिप्रश्नेन सेवया।
उपदेक्ष्यन्ति ते ज्ञानं ज्ञानिनस्तत्त्वदर्शिनः ।।३४।।

34. "Obtain that knowledge (from sages) through reverence, inquiry and innocent solicitation, and the sages who are aware of reality will initiate you into it."

यज्ज्ञात्वा न पुनर्मोहमेवं यास्यसि पाण्डव।
येन भूतान्यशेषेण द्रक्ष्यस्यात्मन्यथो मयि।।३५।।

35. "Knowing which, O son of Pandu, you will never again be a prey like this to attachment, and equipped with this knowledge you will see all beings within yourself and then within me."

अपि चेदसि पापेभ्यः सर्वेभ्यः पापकृत्तमः।
सर्वं ज्ञानप्लवेनैव वृजिनं सन्तरिष्यसि।।३६।।

36. "Even if you are the most heinous sinner, the ark of knowledge will carry you safely across all evils."

यथैधांसि समिद्धोऽग्निर्भस्मसात्कुरुतेऽर्जुन।
ज्ञानाग्निः सर्वकर्माणि भस्मसात्कुरुते तथा।।३७।।

37. "As the blazing fire reduces fuel to ashes, O Arjuna, so does the fire of knowledge reduce all karma to ashes."

Pauri - 8

Explanation

Guru Nanak in this Pauri reveals the benefit of hearing, listening and contemplating the name of Almighty. He emphasizes that getting one's mind and intellect completely merged/associated in the divine words of Almighty, makes him thought less and he becomes one/ merge with Him. Listening is the most difficult activity. However, it is possible with His grace when the attention/concentration is completely merged with the Self and when there is no other thought in the mind. Listening the glory of Almighty is possible when there is complete silence in mind. Also, listening with depth of attention makes the mind silent under the influence of the effective vibrations of the divine words. It changes the complete personality of an individual if he learns the art of listening. Listening is the gateway to higher divine path. The effect of listening forces one to contemplate and finally this makes him to follow the sayings of the Almighty, and thus wisdom and intellect develops. Also, this develops the complete inner silence, which develops the intuition and life force climbs up to the tenth gate through the Sahasara Chakra and from where it enters the gateway to abode and one becomes self realized in due course.. By this process of mergence, a devotee is raised to the higher spiritual level of self- realized saints, dummy Gods, Peers, Sidhas with all divine virtues to such a extend that what he thinks and utters become true. He develops the capabilities to know past, future and miseries of the creatures, and means to overcome their problems.

This process of deep self-realization reveals secrets of the nature to him intuitively. He will know how Almighty has supported the earth and sky, and how by the mercy of God different continents, planets and life in deep earth and ocean smoothly co-exist

To a God self realized person who has been raised to such a high level, death does not scare him. He becomes as perfect as God Himself, and as God is fearless of death so becomes he.

Guru Nanak Ji says that His devotee is always in joy; Almighty keeps joy in the heart of His devotees and gradually extends the joy as his devotion towards God is manifested. This is because of the fact that by contemplation, mediation on His name, all miseries of cultivated sins in the present and past lives are burnt in the divine flame of silence and illumination. Hence there is manifestation of joy, which is inexpressible by any means.

Pauri - 9

Explanation

By associating/listening, by concentrating and becoming mentally and intellectually one with the Words/Sayings of the Almighty, one comprehends Shiva, Brahma and Indra. In other words all the three virtues as depicted by these Gods i.e. Sato Guna (by Brahma), Rajo Guna (by Indira) and Tamo Guna (by Shiva) can be transcended in this life and one can become Gunatit (conqueror of all these three virtues), and transformed himself to a man of self-realization.

By this transformation, by achieving the self-realization, even the ignorant person i.e. man of low intellect can become praise worthy in the society. His wisdom super cedes beyond bounds by the glory of Almighty/the Supreme Cosmic Light.

Furthermore, thus by this process of becoming one with the God's name, developing perfect mental silence, one cultivates the Yogic powers and conceives/feels deeply the difference in gross/physical, Suksham /pranic, Mental, Vigyan and Karan /Causal bodies. Also, one develops insight capabilities to learn essence of Sastras, Smritis and Vedas. In other words his intellect crosses the boundaries of learning. He learns by intuition and not by worldly means. He cultivates the qualities of super consciousness. It is the wonderful development in a human life by the grace of Almighty. He develops Godly qualities

Says Nanak, with the miraculous power of the listening of divine glory and getting merge in that, all miseries and sins are annihilated in the life of a devotee. His level of development is beyond description.

Equivalent Verses of Srimad Bhagavad Gita (Pauri 8-9)

Chapter 18

In Truth Do I Promise Thee: Thou Shalt Attain Me

Summary of the Gita's Message: How God-Realization is attained (Verses 63-71)

इति ते ज्ञानमाख्यातं गुह्याद्गुह्यतरं मया ।
विमृश्यैतदशेषेण यथेच्छसि तथा कुरु ।।६३।।

63. "Thus have I imparted to you the knowledge which is the most mysterious of all abstruse learning; so reflect well on the whole of it (and then) you may do as you wish."

स्सर्वगुह्यतमं भूय: शृणु मे परमं वच: ।
इष्टोऽसि मे दृढमिति ततो वक्ष्यामि ते हितम् ।।६४।।

64."Listen yet again to my most secret words, indeed felicitous, that I am going to speak to you because you are the dearest to me."

मन्मना भव मद्भक्तो मद्याजी मां नमस्कुरु ।
मामेवैष्यसि सत्यं ते प्रतिजाने प्रियोऽसि मे ।।६५।।

65. "I give you my sincere pledge, because you are so dear to me, that you must attain to me if you keep me in mind, adore me, worship me, and bow in obeisance to me."

सर्वधर्मान्परित्यज्य मामेकं शरणं व्रज ।
अहं त्वा सर्वपापेभ्यो मोक्षयिष्यामि मा शुच: ।।६६।।

66. "Grieve not, for I shall free you from all sins if you abandon all other obligations (dharm) and seek refuge in me alone."

इदं ते नातपस्काय नाभक्ताय कदाचन।
न चाशुश्रूषवे वाच्यं न च मां योऽभ्यसूयति।।६७।।

67. "This (the Geeta) which has been articulated for you must never be made known to one who is bereft of penance, devotion, and of willingness to listen, as also to one who speaks ill of me."

य इमं परमं गुह्यं मद्भक्तेष्वभिधास्यति।
भक्तिं मयि परां कृत्वा मामेवैष्यत्यसंशयः।।६८।।

68. "The one who, with firm devotion to me, imparts this most secret teaching of my worshippers will doubtlessly attain to me."

न च तस्मान्मनुष्येषु कश्चिन्मे प्रियकृत्तमः।
भविता न च मे तस्मादन्यः प्रियतरो भुवि।।६९।।

69. "Neither is there among mankind any doer who is dearer to me than this man, nor will there by any in the world who is dearer to me than him."

अध्येष्यते च य इमं धर्म्यं संवादमावयोः।
ज्ञानयज्ञेन तेनाहमिष्टः स्यामिति मे मतिः।।७०।।

70. "And it is my belief that I shall have been worshipped through the yagya of knowledge by one who makes a thorough study of this sacred dialogue between us."

श्रद्धावाननसूयश्च शृणुयादपि यो नरः।
सोऽपि मुक्तः शुभाँल्लोकान्प्राप्नुयात्पुण्यकर्मणाम्।।७१।।

71. ''Even he will be freed from sins who just hears it (the Geeta) with devoutness and without any ill will, and he will secure the worlds of the righteous."

Pauri - 10

Suniye Sat Santokh Gian

Suniye Athsath Ka Ishnan

Suniye Par Par Pave Maan

Suniye Lage Sahaj Dhyan

Nanak Bhagtan Sada Vigaas

Suniye Dookh Paap Ka Naas

Explanation

By associating/ listening deeply and becoming one with the divine Words/glory, one understands Truth, the changeless power of Almighty, essence of the natural secrets and his life becomes contended, without any material desires. He becomes wise with self-realization since he could establish his energies through communication from the tenth gate in his fore head with the cosmic energies with his super consciousness by becoming perfectly silent in his thoughts. His entire actions are governed by the command of Almighty.

With this achievement, one earns merits of spiritual baths at the sixty-eight holy places of pilgrimages existing in India. It clearly brings out that when spiritual life force by meditation /deep listening of divine glory merges through Sahashara with Cosmic energies, it give divine fruits to a devotee equivalent to that of dip in large number of holy places. In other words, one needs not to go and take hectic journey and put efforts for holy dip. Deep attention and merging with the divine glory fetches all the benefits being present at home.

Furthermore, hearing the divine sayings with complete attention in a thoughtless state by a devotee, gives him much more honor than reading books and reproducing their contents. This process leads to a state of Sahaj Meditation, which comes naturally without any external efforts and means. The pre-requisite for a devotee to get absorbed in meditation, is to be able to focus and concentrate on the divine glory i.e. listening with attention the glory of Almighty in a thoughtless state from the origin from where the divine words are generated. Except God everything else is mutable and as such natural meditation is only possible on Almighty by listening to His holy Words in the thoughtless state.

Says Guru Nanak Ji, with the mergence in the divine glory, all miseries and sins of a real devotee are annihilated, and all kinds of spiritual and material progress are assured/granted.

Pauri - 11

Explanation

By associating deeply with the glory of the Lord, a devotee takes a deeper dip in the ocean of virtuous activities of great divine values, which cannot be expressed. By following the divine path of mergence in His glory, one acquires Sheikh's wisdom, Peer's virtue and sovereignty.

By mergence in the divinity by devotion, even the blind (ignorant) finds the way to move in right direction in life and ignorant becomes wise. In other words, human senses are surpassed by developed intuition by mergence in His grace and to be one with His glory. The knowledge of the ocean like world becomes so meager and one is easily able to know all universal mysteries, and thus the Unfathomable comes as close as hand. There is no comparison of accomplishment achieved in life of human being by chanting the glory of Almighty and getting fully merged in it.

Says Nanak, with the divine word/name pervading in the thinking of a devotee, the devotee is always in joy, and all his miseries and sins are annihilated. And thus, by one's association with the holy Word, and getting merge in His glory, one acquires a distinct poise thinking and is fulfilled with inexpressible infinite joy.

Equivalent Verses of Srimad Bhagavad Gita (Pauri 10-11)

Chapter 6

Permanent Shelter In Spirit Through Yoga Meditation

Attaining Self-Mastery and Control of the Mind (verses 20-32)

यत्रोपरमते चित्तं निरुद्धं योगसेवया ।
यत्र चैवात्मनात्मानं पश्यन्नात्मनि तुष्यति ।।२०।।

20. "In the state in which even the yog-restrained mind is dissolved by a direct perception of God, he (the worshipper) rests contented in his Self."

सुखमात्यन्तिकं यत्तद्बुद्धिग्राह्यमतीन्द्रियम् ।
वेत्ति यत्र न चैवायं स्थितश्चलति तत्त्वतः ।।२१।।

21. "After knowing God, he (the yogi) dwells for ever and unwavering in the state in which he is blessed with the eternal, sense-transcending joy that can be felt only by a refined and subtle intellect; and..."

यं लब्ध्वा चापरं लाभं मन्यते नाधिकं ततः ।
यस्मिन्स्थितो न दुःखेन गुरुणापि विचाल्यते ।।२२।।

22. "In this state, in which he believes that there can be no greater good than the ultimate peace he has found in God, he is unshaken by even the direst of all griefs."

तं विद्याद् दुःखसंयोगवियोगं योगसञ्ज्ञितम् ।
स निश्चयेन योक्तव्यो योगोऽनिर्विण्णचेतसा ।।२३।।

23. "It is a duty to practise this yog, untouched by miseries of the world, with vigour and determination, and without a sense of ennui."

सङ्कल्पप्रभवान्कामांस्त्यक्त्वा सर्वानशेषतः।
मनसैवेन्द्रियग्रामं विनियम्य समन्ततः।।२४।।

24. "Abandoning all desire, lust, and attachment, and pulling in by an exercise of the mind the numerous senses from all sides, -"

शनैः शनैरुपरमेद्बुद्ध्या धृतिगृहीतया।
आत्मसंस्थं मनः कृत्वा न किञ्चिदपि चिन्तयेत्।।२५।।

25. "His intellect should also rein in the mind firmly and make it contemplate nothing except God and, thus step by step, he should proceed towards the attainment of final liberation."

यतो यतो निश्चरति मनश्चञ्चलमस्थिरम्।
ततस्ततो नियम्यैतदात्मन्येव वशं नयेत्।।२६।।

26. "Doing away with the causes that make the inconstant and fickle wander among worldly objects, he should devote his mind to God alone."

प्रशान्तमनसं ह्येनं योगिनं सुखमुत्तमम्।
उपैति शान्तरजसं ब्रह्मभूतमकल्मषम्।।२७।।

27. "The most sublime happiness is the lot of the yogi whose mind is at peace, who is free from evil, whose passion and moral blindness have been dispelled, and who has become one with God."

युञ्जन्नेवं सदात्मानं योगी विगतकल्मषः।
सुखेन ब्रह्मसंस्पर्शमत्यन्तं सुखमश्नुते।।२८।।

28. "Thus constantly dedicating his Self to God, the immaculate yogi experiences the eternal bliss of realization.."

सर्वभूतस्थमात्मानं सर्वभूतानि चात्मनि ।
ईक्षते योगयुक्तात्मा सर्वत्र समदर्शनः ॥२९॥

29. "The worshipper, whose Self has achieved the state of yog and who sees all with an equal eye, beholds his own Self in all beings and all beings in his Self."

यो मां पश्यति सर्वत्र सर्वं च मयि पश्यति ।
तस्याहं न प्रणश्यामि स च मे न प्रणश्यति ॥३०॥

30. "From the man, who sees me as the Soul in all beings and all beings in me (Vasudev) , 3 I am not hidden and he is not hidden from me."

सर्वभूतस्थितं यो मां भजत्येकत्वमास्थितः ।
सर्वथा वर्तमानोऽपि स योगी मयि वर्तते ॥३१॥

31. 'The even-minded yogi (who has known the unity of the individual Soul and the Supreme Spirit) who adores me (Vasudev), the Soul in all beings, abides in me no matter whatever he does."

आत्मौपम्येन सर्वत्र समं पश्यति योऽर्जुन ।
सुखं वा यदि वा दुःखं स योगी परमो मतः ॥३२॥

32. 'The worshipper, O Arjun, who perceives all things as identical and regards happiness and sorrow as identical, is thought to be the most accomplished yogi."

Pauri - 12

Explanation

In this Pauri Guru Nanak Ji has explained the depth of the wonderful philosophy of God-realization. As it looks, it is not that simple Pauri. It is extremely difficult to understand/comprehend the dynamic nature of mind or it may be said that those, who have firm faith in Almighty, their mental status is beyond expression. Furthermore, who contemplates deeply in various dimensions, it is all the more complex to gauge their thinking. Still more, it can be said that the status of an individual is not accessible when he has transcended the mind. It means when, there is no more mind, and the mind is surpassed/transcended. In such situation, one is directly with the Almighty, the Supreme Cosmic Light. He becomes Jeewan Mukta and part and parcel of Almighty force, the God. No body on earth can discuss his status and even perceive him.

Any body, who, tries to do this, can never succeed. He has to repent after putting lot of efforts to proceed in this direction. Still, he can never come to any conclusion regarding his status, his achievement and his wisdom. In other words it is beyond the mental capacity of a common human being even to perceive the stature and level of enlightenment of Jeewan Mukta, a self-realized soul.

It is not practicable to write his virtues and capabilities on paper. His wisdom and capabilities are like Deep Ocean; these cannot be put in writings. All efforts done seriously in this direction, will finally be in vain since infinite can not be made finite to express on paper and even to contemplate. Every moment an individual will feel to deduce and express more, there will not be end to all this. Finally, one may conclude that ocean cannot be put in any vessel existing in this world. It has no boundary and limitation. Great thinker and philosopher cannot express the one who has transcended the mind.

God and His name are above Maya, the delusion. The only one, who has succeeded to immerge himself in His name/ divinity by the grace and blessings of Almighty, can transcend his mind, he only can understand, feel his omnipresent name, but cannot express Him by any means since He is beyond mind and human senses. So, by any physical means, Almighty, and the devotee, who has transcended his mind, are beyond expression and description.

Pauri - 13

Explanation

Under deep contemplation, meditation, when the mind is annihilated, and the complete attention is bounded with the internal energies, an era of silence appears in the mental frame and vacuum reign is established in the consciousness. In this thoughtless state intuition develops and the mind then conceives the deep secrets in the state of, super consciousness, which discloses universal secrets on the mental consciousness. Thus, the deep mysteries of the cosmos get unfolded.

When the mind is annihilated, one never faces disgrace in his life. He is honored and always praise worthy since he gets uplifted from the worldly attachments and operated above the sensuous pleasures. He is always above worldly vices/Vikaras. He is finally graced with the liberation from the wheels of life and death. He becomes Jeewan Mukta being alive in this world. It is because of the fact that every vice/Vikar is in mind and if the mind is annihilated, made to zero level, the trace of such bad tendencies get annealed by it self, and such an uplifted soul gradually becomes perfect in all respects with the blessings of Almighty and come closer and closer to Him. Fear of death is completely annihilated. He achieves all divine virtues by the annihilation of mind, which becomes under his control by his efforts and God's grace. Physical death never bothers him.

By the grace of God, and by the blessing of His pure name and divinity, he reaches to the highest state of spirituality. Such a person knows the joy of importance of mindless state by the deep process of contemplation, meditation and becoming unison with His consciousness. This is the highest achievement of human life in his life span, and it is beyond human efforts and it is the highest achievement by the grace of Almighty. However, it is feasible when one becomes effortless after exhausting all his efforts to be self-realized. It is the state of enlightenment.

Pauri - 14

Manne Marag Thak Na Paye

Manne Pat Siun Pargat Jaye

Manne Mag Na Chale Panth

Manne Dharam Seti Sanbandha

Aisa Naam Niranjan Hoye

Je Ko Mann Jane Mann Koye

Explanation

For such a person, who is capable of having annihilated the mind in real and perfect sense in his life, there occurs no problem of any kind to him in this transient world. Even if there are a few problems, he takes them happily as the wish of Almighty and remains in perfect joy. He takes birth in the glamour of Almighty with respect and leaves his body after living the life honorably in God's grace. He earns glory and honor in his life; he lives in divine glory and immerges only in His glory with perfect joy.

He does not follow any particular religious league in his life, and he never follows the path of religious strictness. For him the religion is the way of life to arrive at ultimate self-realization. All religions finally immerge to the same ocean of realization. He never flows with the religious paths, but follows the essence of religions and establishes the close intrinsic relation with core and ultimate purpose of religion. He never criticizes any religion and considers all religions are alike since a religion can follow any path but ultimate goal of all the religions is the same. He does not believe to follow any cult and establish himself with the physical Guru. For him the Almighty is the beginning and the end and love to Him is supreme. He lives and dies for the supreme reality, Cosmic Light, the Almighty.

More and more if one annihilates his mind by the process of mergence by listening the divine glory, he gets uplifted towards the supreme path of spirituality. He then only understands and feels from the depth of his heart the importance of the glory of chanting His divine name. Such a Word (*Naam*) of Almighty is *Niranjan- pure and perfect that makes a devotee the same (pure & perfect) in due course, and it is* realized only by devotee's faith after total immergence in the divine glory of His name (Naam-by chanting His name) without any other thought.

Pauri - 15

Explanation

The importance of the annihilation of the mind is further continued. Annihilation of the mind may be understood as its disappearance or in other words self is expanded in totality. This increases spiritual power and only by this one can reach to the doorsteps of liberation. Disappearance of mind dissolves desires and one develops non-attachment/vairagah, which increases gradually with time following the art of annihilation of mind by mergence in divine glory (through chanting His name), and thus one gets liberated and becomes Jeewan Mukta in this life span. Such a liberated one guides the society and own family to follow the path of divine glory to climb to the ladder of self-realization.

Following the divine path and divine way of living, both master and disciple get liberated, and get the fruits of self-realization. Master with the art of self-realization having fully accomplished, helps disciple with his enlightenment, and thus enlightens the disciple also in this life. By chanting the Name/ Naam of the Almighty and getting immerged into it, the Guru/ master assists a devotee to be self-realized in due course.

Guru Nanak Ji depicts, that by following the path of self-realization, one gets all the material benefits in a sahaj way. He need not to run after the material goods, goods come by itself to such a devotee who sincerely put his efforts to realize the God. No occasion in his life ever come that he is deprived of material needs. He never begs rather he gives to the needy. In other words, he never undergoes discomforts by lack of material needs and run after them in this worldly ocean of miseries and troubles. Being with God, one becomes God like. He is raised above the effect of Maya-the delusion by the blessings and grace of Almighty.

The name/glory of the God, and its chanting is without any trace mark of evil effects. Vices remain far away from divine personality who is immerged in the divine glory by annihilation of his mind. He is fit to follow the vertical divine path without any inhibition. The word/Naam of the God becomes Niranjan, pure and perfect to the devotee, and it is realized by his deep faith after getting immerged in the glory of chanting His name (Naam).

Equivalent Verses of Srimad Bhagavad Gita (Pauri 12-15)

Chapter 6

Permanent Shelter In Spriti Through Yoga Meditation

The Lord's Promise: The Persevering Yogi Ultimately is Victorious (Verses 35-47)

असंशयं महाबाहो मनो दुर्निग्रहं चलम्।
अभ्यासेन तु कौन्तेय वैराग्येण च गृह्यते ।।३५।।

35. "The Lord said, 'The mind is, O the mighty-armed, doubtlessly fickle and hard to restrain, but it is disciplined, O son of Kunti, by perseverance of effort and renunciation.'"

असंयतात्मना योगो दुष्प्राप इति मे मतिः।
वश्यात्मना तु यतता शक्योऽवाप्तुमुपायतः ।।३६।।

36. " It is my firm conviction that while the attainment of yog is most difficult for a man who fails to restrain his mind, it is easy for him who is his own master and active in the performance of the required action."

पार्थ नैवेह नामुत्र विनाशस्तस्य विद्यते।
न हि कल्याणकृत्कश्चिद्दुर्गतिं तात गच्छति ।।४०।।

40. "The Lord said, 'This man, O Parth, is destroyed neither in this world nor in the next because, my brother, one who performs good deeds never comes to grief.'"

प्राप्य पुण्यकृतां लोकानुषित्वा शाश्वतीः समाः।
शुचीनां श्रीमतां गेहे योगभ्रष्टोऽभिजायते ।।४१।।

41. "The righteous man who deviates from the path of yog achieves celestial merits and pleasures for countless years after which he is reborn in the house of a virtuous and noble man (or fortunate and thriving man)."

अथवा योगिनामेव कुले भवति धीमताम्।
एतद्धि दुर्लभतरं लोके जन्म यदीदृशम्।।४२।।

42. "Or he is admitted to the family (kul) of discerning yogi and such a birth is truly the most rare in the world."

तत्र तं बुद्धिसंयोगं लभते पौर्वदेहिकम्।
यतते च ततो भूयः संसिद्धौ कुरूनन्दन।।४३।।

43. "He naturally bears with him into his new birth the noble impressions (sanskar) of yog from his previous existence, and by dint of this he strives well for perfection (that comes from the realization of God)."

पूर्वाभ्यासेन तेनैव ह्रियते ह्यवशोऽपि सः।
जिज्ञासुरपि योगस्य शब्दब्रह्मातिवर्तते।।४४।।

44. "Although he is lured by objects Of sense, the merits of his previous life indeed draw him towards God and his aspiration for yog enables him to go beyond the material rewards promised by the Ved."

प्रयत्नाद्यतमानस्तु योगी संशुद्धकिल्बिषः।
अनेकजन्मसंसिद्धस्ततो याति परां गतिम्।।४५।।

45. "The yogi, who has purified his heart and mind through several births by intense meditation and thus rid himself of all sins, attains to the ultimate state of realizing God."

तपस्विभ्योऽधिको योगी ज्ञानिभ्योऽपि मतोऽधिकः।
कर्मिभ्यश्चाधिको योगी तस्माद्योगी भवार्जुन।।४६।।

46. "Since yogi are superior to men who do penance, or men who follow the path of discrimination, or men who desire the fruits of action, O Kurunandan, you should be a doer of selfless action."

योगिनामपि सर्वेषां मद्गतेनान्तरात्मना।
श्रद्धावान्भजते यो मां स मे युक्ततमो मतः।।४७।।

47. "Among all yogi I think that one the best who is dedicated to me and who, abiding in the Self, always adores me."

Pauri - 16

Panch Parvan Panch Pardhan
Panche Pave Darghe Maan
Panche Sohen Dur Rajaan
Panchan Ka Guru Ek Dhiyan
Je Ko Kahe Kare Vichaar
Karte Kai Karne Nahi Shumaar
Dhaul Dharam Daiya Ka Poot
Santokh Thaap Rakhia Jin Soot
Je Ko Bujhe Hovai Sachiaar
Dhaule Ooper Keta Bhaar
Dharti Hore Pare Hore Hore
Tis Te Bhaar Tale Kavan Jore
Jia Jati Ranga Ke Nav
Sabhna Likhia Vuri Kalaam
Ehu Lekha Likhi Jane Koye
Lekha Likhia Keta Hoye
Keta Taan Sualihu Roop
Keti Daat Jane Kaun Koot
Kita Pasao Eko Kavao
Tis Te Hoye Lakh Dariyao
Qudrat Kavan Kahan Vichaar
Varia Na Javan Ek Vaar
Ju Tudh Bhave Sai Bhali Kaar
Tu Sada Salamat Nirankar

Explanation

This Pauri depicts that all those people who are merged in the glory of Almighty by the process of annihilation of their mind, are renowned in the society, are well respected and become leaders in different walks of life in this world. They are honored in spiritual sphere, and the rulers of the regime respect them in their senates. The main reason for all this is their being mentally oneness/mergence with the Almighty/ Cosmic light. The other complex meaning of this Pauri can be understood philosophically as follows:

In a human body, there are five main accepted sense organs, which govern the physical body, are: eyes, nose, ears, tongue and skin. The five important recognized functions of these organs are: to see, smell, and hear, to taste and to touch. Five organs of action, which are duly respected in the divine sphere to execute the body, worldly and divine functions are: hands, feet, tongue, organs of reproduction and evacuation organs. Similarly, five constituents of a human body, are: earth, air, water, fire, and ether. They are universally accepted and when the body is diminished, all these constituents merge with the existing constituents of the Mother Nature. Besides these, there are five Pranas in the body kingdom: namely, Prana, Apana, Samana, Vyana and Udana. These Pranas govern the entire body functions and command great regard since any misbalance of their functioning, make the body unhealthy and sick with time. Furthermore, other abstract governing forces of human body are: mind, heart/Chit/emotion, intellect, ego and soul. Master for all these governing forces and instruments is Almighty, and attention /concentration/mergence in Him is the means by which linkage/ communication can be established with Him to run the human machinery properly with co-ordination of working of all organs, senses and forces with the life force. By due attention, one can smell, can see, can listen and govern entire outward and inner activities of the body. God is the main controller and meditation is the means to interact with Him through the evolution of life force. That is the reason Dhyana/meditation is the Master of the various above activities.

Even if one ventures to reflect and recount the work of Almighty by his knowledge and capability, the Creator's work being infinite, cannot be expressed with the finite intellect. Infinite cannot be assessed by finite sources .No one ever can assess the God work. It is beyond imagination of one's perception and to assess all these must not be the thinking of an individual. Mergence in His glory must be the sole aim of a creature. Only one can imagine His splendid activities by intuition in the thoughtless meditative state

Religious self–realized aspirant knows entirely all the forces acting within him. Religious /spiritual aspirant acts as bull to take entire load of worldly misdeeds of people to allow them to sail/live smoothly on this earth. Mercy is the resultant of spiritual development in his life that originates contentment in his life, which make him happy, full of joy to lead life in the blessing of Almighty under His supreme grace. In other words religious/spiritual man in real sense takes load and acts as load carrying device like a bull, which purify the entire system with his mercy, contentment and other divine qualities and show the way of perfection to lead a peaceful life to the fellow beings. It is proven fact, however difficult to believe that this world is functioning smoothly with all types of disparities because of spiritualism and existence of spiritual power of enlightened persons. Those who conceive this reality, they also become enlightened with time with the spiritual power of the uplifted souls. God-realized people in this world take burden of sinners, uplift them and establish homogeneity in the society, surroundings, and communities. Once this balance is disturbed, the chance to collapse is inevitable.

Furthermore, it is expressed that this universe is magnanimous, The Cosmos is infinite, and even infinite is small world to express its greatness.. There are number of earths, one below the other. No one can count. How these earths, support each earth by which mechanism, and by which force, is miraculous. It is beyond the concept of an individual to apprehend that how magnanimous masses of different earths are being supported.

Creatures of various names and shapes exist on these earths, and in this vast cosmos. All these creatures are manifested by God's words. All these are the result of His glory. To know all this count and write all about this is beyond the capability of a finite human being. Almighty is all-powerful, so glorious and His infinite expanse is everywhere.

What grandeur of bounties, can anyone assess? It is beyond expression. It is by all His mercy and wonder. As the grand is the external cosmos, the similar grandness and infinite force exists within human physical body and psychological mental frame.

The infinite expanse of this universe is by His Will, Where in there are infinite and diverse oceans of Life so diverse that no one can express. Millions of channel of flow of life forces in the entire human system is so complex and mysterious that only Almighty 's infinite wisdom can design and operate His Powerful Nature. "I" am too small to be sacrificed to His grand expanse even once. A human being is so small even to appreciate His glamour, vastness and expanse. Almighty is ever changeless, and living under His wish is the ladder to perfection in one's life. What He likes and does for us is the best.

What pleases Thee is goodness abound

Eternal and Immutable only Thou are around.

Equivalent Verses of Srimad Bhagavad Gita (Pauri 16)

Chapter 15

Purushottama: The Uttermost Being

How Spirit Manifests As the Soul (Verses 7-15)

ममैवांशो जीवलोके जीवभूतः सनातनः।
मनःषष्ठानीन्द्रियाणि प्रकृतिस्थानि कर्षति।।७।।

7. "The immortal Soul in the body is a part of mine and it is he who attracts the five senses and the sixth-the mind-that dwell in nature."

शरीरं यदवाप्नोति यच्चाप्युत्क्रामतीश्वरः।
गृहीत्वैतानि संयाति वायुर्गन्धानिवाशयात्।।८।।

8. "Like the wind carrying a scent from its source, the Soul that is lord of the body also bears along with him the senses and the mind from its previous body and assumes a new one."

श्रोत्रं चक्षुः स्पर्शनं च रसनं घ्राणमेव च।
अधिष्ठाय मनश्चायं विषयानुपसेवते।।९।।

9. "Governing the senses of hearing, sight, touch, taste, smell and also the mind, he (the Soul) experiences objects through them."

उत्क्रामन्तं स्थितं वापि भुञ्जानं वा गुणान्वितम्।
विमूढा नानुपश्यन्ति पश्यन्ति ज्ञानचक्षुषः।।१०।।

10. "The ignorant are unaware of the Soul, endowed with the three properties and departing from the body or dwelling in it and enjoying objects; only they who have eyes of wisdom discern him."

यतन्तो योगिनश्चैनं पश्यन्त्यात्मन्यवस्थितम् ।
यतन्तोऽप्यकृतात्मानो नैनं पश्यन्त्यचेतसः ।।११।।

11. "Yogi know the essence of the Soul dwelling in their heart, but the unknowing who have not purified themselves (of evils) fail to see him even after much endeavour."

यदादित्यगतं तेजो जगद्भासयतेऽखिलम् ।
यच्चन्द्रमसि यच्चाग्नौ तत्तेजो विद्धि मामकम् ।।१२।।

12. "Know that the radiance of the sun that lights up the world, and of the moon and fire, is my own effulgence."

गामाविश्य च भूतानि धारयाम्यहमोजसा ।
पुष्णामि चौषधीः सर्वाः सोमो भूत्वा रसात्मकः ।।१३।।

13. "Permeating the earth, I support all beings with my radical energy and like the ambrosial moon, I provide the sap that nourishes all plants."

अहं वैश्वानरो भूत्वा प्राणिनां देहमाश्रितः ।
प्राणापानसमायुक्तः पचाम्यन्नं चतुर्विधम् ।।१४।।

14. "I am the fire, possessed of pran and apan, within the body of all living beings that consumes the four kinds of food."

सर्वस्य चाहं हृदि सन्निविष्टो मत्तः स्मृतिर्ज्ञानमपोहनं च ।
वेदैश्च सर्वैरहमेव वेद्यो वेदान्तकृद्वेदविदेव चाहम् ।।१५।।

15. "Seated in the heart of all beings, I am their memory and knowledge and also the strength that overcomes all impediments; I am that which is worthy of being apprehended by the Ved; and I verily am the author of the Vedant as well as their knower."

Pauri - 17

Explanation

This and the next Pauri reveals the incomprehensible diversity of God's creation. Guru Nanak Ji says it is wonderful mystery of Almighty, and all this is due to His will. This Pauri depicts that there are infinite ways for the recitation of His name and there are countless means to express the love and devotion towards Almighty. Uncounted ways of worships, prayers and atonements exist, and devotees select as per their inner choice and temperament. There is no way one can count types of penances, which devotees offer to the Lord. There are countless creatures in the universe who devote their life for pleasing the Almighty by various means of chanting/reciting His divine name, worship, love and do rigorous penance for the Self-realization.

Furthermore, there are infinite number of holy books on devotion and illustrating glory of His name, which devotees read with utmost devotion and recite loudly the different hymn of recitation given in the ancient Indian religious books, the Vedas. Devotees implement various yogic techniques to achieve the self-realization in an accelerated way by evolving life force in the pranic system of the body, and then uplifting this divine energy to the forehead on passing through various Chakras to the tenth gate at Sahasara. By this process automatically dispassion/Vairagah develops in their mind and they cease to find any happiness in worldly materials and gains. Such devotees become indifferent to the worldly affairs, detachment is developed in their heart, and their sole aim of life revolve around towards realization of God.

There are countless devotees in this universe, those who praise divine virtues in various forms and develop initially divine knowledge by deep contemplation, and later by becoming thoughtless. They develop intuition. And finally they succeed to merge in His glory and divine virtues. In this way various devotees get transformed themselves in the category of saints and million of such saints transformed to much higher level of spiritualism where they develop the capability to give, to donate to the needy, and their heart is filled with mercy to the fellow being. Gradually they become highly pious and benevolent from the core of their heart with time.

Million of courageous warriors worship Him. And uncounted devotees turns to become warriors to fight evil in the society and they happily scarify to fight evil forces and uplift society and defend the Nation from enemy. Besides this, in time of peace such devotees observe silence of mind by keeping their senses under control and annihilate their mind to merge in nectar of meditation to be with Him uninterruptly.

It is impossible to think and describe the great expanse of His blessings on creatures. I, a humble being, even once cannot show my gratitude for His uncounted grace and blessing on us .Oh, Almighty, what you do for us, is the best. However, we may immediately do not recognize His blessings. He is changeless, omnipresent, without any shape and frame, I always pray for His glory to get merge with Him.

In short, it is said:

What can express Thy Powerful Nature
May "I" be sacrificed to this at once
what pleases Thee is goodness abound
Eternal and Immutable only Thou are around.

Equivalent Verses of Srimad Bhagavad Gita (Pauri 17)

Chapter 17

Three Kinds Of Faith

Three Patterns of Worship (Verses 1-6)

ये शास्त्रविधिमुत्सृज्य यजन्ते श्रद्धयान्विताः ।
तेषां निष्ठा तु का कृष्ण सत्त्वमाहो रजस्तमः ॥१॥

1. "Arjun said, What, O Krishn, is the property-sattwa, rajas, or tamas of persons who albeit worship with faith but in disregard of the scriptural ordinance ?' "

त्रिविधा भवति श्रद्धा देहिनां सा स्वभावजा ।
सात्त्विकी राजसी चैव तामसी चेति तां शृणु ॥२॥

2. "The Lord said, 'Listen to me on how the faith arising from people's innate nature, too, is of three kinds, virtuous, impassioned, and blind.'"

सत्त्वानुरूपा सर्वस्य श्रद्धा भवति भारत ।
श्रद्धामयोऽयं पुरुषो यो यच्छ्रद्धः स एव सः ॥३॥

3. "Since the faith of all people, O Bharat, is according to their inherent propensity and man is reverent, he is what his faith is."

यजन्ते सात्त्विका देवान्यक्षरक्षांसि राजसाः ।
प्रेतान्भूतगणांश्चान्ये यजन्ते तामसा जनाः ॥४॥

4. "While the virtuous worship gods and the impassioned and morally blind worship yaksh and demons, they who are blinded by ignorance worship ghosts and nature-spirits."

अशास्त्रविहितं घोरं तप्यन्ते ये तपो जना: ।
दम्भाहङ्कारसंयुक्ताः कामरागबलान्विताः ।।५।।
कर्शयन्तः शरीरस्थं भूतग्राममचेतसः ।
मां चैवान्तःशरीरस्थं तान्विद्ध्यासुरनिश्चयान् ।।६।।

5-6. "Mark you that they who undergo terrible self-mortification without scriptural sanction and are afflicted with hypocrisy and arrogance besides lust, attachment, and vanity of power, and who wear out not only the elements that form their bodies bur also me who dwells in their Souls, are ignorant men with evil disposition."

Pauri -18

Asankh Moorakh Andh Ghor

Asankh Chor Haram Khor

Asankh Amar Kar Jahi Jor

Asankh Galvadh Hatya Kamahin

Asankh Paapi Paap Kar Jahin

Asankh Kuriar Kure Phirahin

Asankh Malecch Mal Bhakh Khahin

Asankh Nindak Siri Karhin Bhaar

Nanak Neech Kare Vichhaar

Varia Na Javan Ek Vaar

Ju Tudh Bhave Sai Bhali Kaar

Tu Sada Salamat Nirankar

Explanation

This Pauri explains further the diversity of God's creation. Countless unsocial works are discussed here along with the countless unsocial elements existing in the society, their nature, way of life and their sins. There are countless fools, ignorant people, spiritually blind, thieves, swindlers, thriving on spoils, and are parasites, which survive on other's income. There are varieties of unsocial immortalize brutal force apart from those who rule with cruelty, and harass the innocent people around them. There are countless murderers, those who earn their livelihood with cruel and brutal activities in the society. There is no end to such countless sinners whose activity is to commit sins, and cultivate only sins in their life. Uncounted people speak false in every sphere of life in all the activities as if to speak untruth is truth for them. Actually falsehood is their way of living. Truth just cannot come out from their mouth. All their activism is based on untruth and it is not possible to recognize them. Innocent people get trapped, the way they speak untruth as if they are the only truthful people existing in the society.

Furthermore, uncounted masses in the society consume wrong food and develop wrong desires. They live on animal meat, which gives improper thoughts and take excessive energy for digestion. In this way their thinking pattern is disturbed. In the long run, excessive desires of sex and greed develop, which is accompanied by various health hazards and unscrupulous wrong mental tendencies like anger, egoism and uncontrolled bad habits. They develop the habits of insulting others without any proper reason. It is said, those who insult others, clean the sins by their tongue. In other words as if such people who insult others, take their sins unknowingly. Such people are filled mentally with sins and neither can think in right direction and nor can speak truth.

In short, there is class of people in the society, which are completely Tamasic in nature. They are rude, stubborn, ignorant, cruel, brutal, liars, sinners and all their activities go in the unconscious state of mind without any understanding of right and wrong. Divine thoughts and goodness do not affect them. They are full of egoism and do not consider any body equal to them. Their food is Tamasic and so their nature is full of vices. They are real enemies of the society. Only physical punishment to them, can create fear and improve them to some extend. Good preaching, good thoughts and analysis do not influence them at all. Instead they become the enemy of all those who try to show them proper way of living. They can only be improved by their own wish and by the grace of God if really some strong daunted incidence touches the core of their heart. It is indeed a very rare phenomenon that such people in the society are improved in this birth.

The inner meaning of this Pauri is really highlights the innermost secret tendencies of human mind. This depicts that human mind is completely attached with the sensual pleasures. Mind is completely ignorant and is trapped with greediness, parasitic nature, and full of cruelty, brutality, and selfishness and always hurt others for their own gains. They commit sins on every occasion with unscrupulous mental tendencies. This is basic reason that one has to undergo all miseries of life as the resultant of his own sins under cause and effect theory of the spiritual science. His egoistic inner nature because of wrong mental tendencies, force him to commit sins of highest order for which he has to repent when he undergoes mental trials. Such people are enemies of the self because of their bad inbuilt mental nature/tendencies due to the past actions, and harm themselves by the reactions of their mental sins by the theory of cause and effect in the same way as unscrupulous people of society has to undergo legal trials in the society by their physical misdeeds.

Guru Nanak Ji with all humility counts himself with the categories of such sinners. As per Him, by self efforts and God grace one can follow the way to the perfection to reform himself to become the divine in this life to overcome all his miseries. He says even once he cannot show his gratitude towards Almighty for His might blessings and grace on the creatures. He admits that the wish of the Almighty must be accepted and will be the best for such humble creatures like us. Almighty is omnipresent, omnipotent and Changeless without any form and shape, and beyond time-the deathless.

Equivalent Verses of Srimad Bhagavad Gita (Pauri 18)

Chapter 17

Three Kinds Of Faith

Three Classes of Food (Verses 7-10)

आहारस्त्वपि सर्वस्य त्रिविधो भवति प्रियः।
यज्ञस्तपस्तथा दानं तेषां भेदमिमं श‍ृणु ।।७।।

7. "Listen to me (as I tell you) the distinction between the three kinds of yagya, penance, and alms, that are like the three kinds of food relished according to individual taste."

आयुः सत्त्वबलारोग्यसुखप्रीतिविवर्धनाः।
रस्याः स्निग्धाः स्थिरा हृद्या आहाराः सात्त्विकप्रियाः ।।८।।

8. "Food that is naturally pleasing and conducive to life, intellect, strength, sound health, happiness, and satisfaction besides being savoury, tender, and durable is loved by the virtuous."

कट्वम्ललवणात्युष्णतीक्ष्णरूक्षविदाहिनः।
आहारा राजसस्येष्टा दुःखशोकामयप्रदाः ।।९।।

9. "Bitter, sour, salty, too hot, pungent, rough, and acidic food that gives rise to sorrow, worries, and illness, is preferred by the passionate."

यातयामं गतरसं पूति पर्युषितं च यत्।
उच्छिष्टमपि चामेध्यं भोजनं तामसप्रियम् ।।१०।।

10. "Food that is half-cooked, unsavoury, odorous, stale, leftover, and defiled is liked by men with a dull sensibility."

Pauri - 19

Asankh Nav Asankh Thanv

Agam Agam Asankh Loa

Asankh Kahe Sir Bhaar Hoye

Akhari Naam Akhari Salah

Akhari Gyan Geet Gun Gah

Akhari Likhan Bolan Baan

Akharan Sir Sanjog Vakhaan

Jin Eh Likhe Tis Sir Nahin

Jiv Phurmae Tiv Tiv Pahin

Jeta Kita Teta Naun

Vin Naven Nahi Ko Thaun

Qudrat Kavan Kahan Vichaar

Varia Na Javan Ek Vaar

Ju Tudh Bhave Sai Bhali Kaar

Tu Sada Salamat Nirankar

Explanation

In continuation with Pauri 17 and 18, where picture of countless types of good and worst social elements have been brought before the universe, in this Pauri infinite unimaginable magnificence of the Almighty is expressed so that worldly people must conceive clearly that divine force is omnipotent and powerful to take any action to rectify the situation. And by following the divine path one gets the appropriate chances to uplift his life and could overcome and face the miseries of his life.

As there are thousand names of God, recited and listed in Vishnu sahastranama, but still there are countless names of the God, which are beyond physical count. There are countless places and realms where He/Almighty resides. He is omnipresent and omniscient. There are countless universes where in He exists and it is beyond imagination to reach there. Even to use word 'infinite' i.e. countless for Him, is too small to express His existence. Even to say countless is sin for a human being. This word "infinite" is not proper to use for Almighty. To use this word creates a type of undue burden for devotee, to express His omnipresence characteristic since there is no other existing vocabulary to project Him. To use any word created by human being is disgrace to be used to express His glory and potential. He is beyond the boundaries of the word.

Further to express Him by words, since there are no other means/ways, so only words are used to express His knowledge and virtues. Even to pray and express His glory, words are used. The songs to praise Him are through words. Divine knowledge by devotees are expressed through words. Spoken words are used to write about His glory. Words are ordinance of our destiny. Divine fate of an individual is expressed by words only. Every expression revolves around words. But what so ever is written about Him, nothing is adequate. He is free and beyond words. The laws of the universe do not bind him. He is beyond and much beyond all means of human writing, expressions, thoughts, words, and cannot be approached by these means. What so ever Almighty wishes, only that is ought to happen. All creatures of the universe receive and undergo trials, as per His command. He is supreme and is governed by His own Self.

In addition, if there is a form, then it exists only with a name. Similarly if there is a word, it must manifest itself into a form. This is pure science. Man just cannot think without words. Man cannot even be silent for long without words. And every word that we comprehend, write or speak associates with it a form. This can be easily examined/tested/experienced by one self by simply uttering words at random. One will see that with each word an image springs from within the storehouse of our memory and consciousness. And when the name and form do not "co-exist", then we find ourselves confused and lost.

God has created this whole universe, and it is His own physical expression in various shapes and forms. There is no place without Him any where in this universe. He is present in tiny atom, and even in an electron and space around in a formless form. He is ever vigilant. No body can ever conceive how he is present everywhere in no form and in all the forms. Guru Nanak dev Ji expresses that we, the human being, are too insignificant to express even once our gratitude for His grace and blessings on us. Almighty is changeless, formless, beyond time and is omnipresent. To live under His supervision and fully surrendering to His wish, without any mental desire of our own, is the supreme trouble free way of human existence. To follow His command is the best way for us to lead a human life to arrive at the destination of God-realization.

Equivalent Verses of Srimad Bhagavad Gita (Pauri 19)

Chapter 17

Three Kinds Of Faith

Three Grades of Spiritual Practices (Verses 11-19)

अफलाकाङ्क्षिभिर्यज्ञो विधिदृष्टो य इज्यते।
यष्टव्यमेवेति मनः समाधाय स सात्त्विकः ।।११।।

11. "Yagya that has scriptural sanction and the performance of which is an obligation, is fitting and auspicious when it is practised by persons with intent minds who aspire to no reward."

अभिसन्धाय तु फलं दम्भार्थमपि चैव यत्।
इज्यते भरतश्रेष्ठ तं यज्ञं विद्धि राजसम् ।।१२।।

12. "And, O the unequalled among Bharat, be it known to you that the yagya which is embarked upon for mere ostentation, or even with a view to some reward, is contaminated by passion and moral blindness."

विधिहीनमसृष्टान्नं मन्त्रहीनमदक्षिणम्।
श्रद्धाविरहितं यज्ञं तामसं परिचक्षते।।१३।।

13. "Devoid of scriptural sanction and powerless to invoke the Supreme Spirit as well as to restrain the mind, the yagya that is engaged in without a sense of total sacrifice and faith is said to be demoniacal"

देवद्विजगुरुप्राज्ञपूजनं शौचमार्जवम्।
ब्रह्मचर्यमहिंसा च शारीरं तप उच्यते।।१४।।

14. "Adoration of God, the twice-born, the teacher-preceptor, and of the learned, along with having the qualities of innocence, uprightness, chastity, and disinclination to violence-are said to be penance of the body."

अनुद्वेगकरं वाक्यं सत्यं प्रियहितं च यत्।
स्वाध्यायाभ्यसनं चैव वाङ्मयं तप उच्यते।।१५।।

15. "And utterance that does not agitate but is soothing, propitious, and truthful, and which is but an exercise in the study of Ved, in remembrance of the Supreme Being, and in Self-contemplation, is said to be the penance of speech."

मनःप्रसादः सौम्यत्वं मौनमात्मविनिग्रहः।
भावसंशुद्धिरित्येतत्तपो मानसमुच्यते।।१६।।

16. "Affable temperament, tranquillity, silent meditation, self-possession, inner purity, and the like are said to be penance of the mind."

श्रद्धया परया तप्तं तपस्तत्त्रिविधं नरैः।
अफलाकाङ्क्षिभिर्युक्तैः सात्त्विकं परिचक्षते।।१७।।

17. "The threefold types of penance undergone with utmost faith by selfless persons who do not desire any fruit thereof is said to be truly righteous."

सत्कारमानपूजार्थं तपो दम्भेन चैव यत्।
क्रियते तदिह प्रोक्तं राजसं चलमध्रुवम्।।१८।।

18. "And if undergone with the purpose of gaining homage, honour, and adoration, or for mere display, penance is unsteady and ephemeral, and is said to have the property of rajas."

मूढग्राहेणात्मनो यत्पीडया क्रियते तपः।
परस्योत्सादनार्थं वा तत्तामसमुदाहृतम्।।१९।।

19. "The penance that is undertaken out of mere stupid stubbornness or to hurt others is said to be diabolical."

Pauri - 20

Explanation

In this Pauri Guru Nanak Ji, using examples from our daily life explains how a confused, chaotic and imbalanced mental state can be brought to peace and harmony, and how a sincere devotee who follows the path of life upright can dissolve/ remove the accumulated sins of life.

He explains with routine examples that dusty hands, feet and body get cleaned when washed with water. Soap washes cloths spoiled by excreta for reuse. Ordinary water does not help to clean such filthy cloths and not the harmful germs of excreta can be removed by this way. Good detergent is required for such cleaning to use the cloths hygienically for the forthcoming use. Similarly when human mind gets taunted with sinful deeds even by thinking ill of others and having chaste-less thoughts, and with various other types of mental vices, it can be purified only through reciting the divine name i.e. by Japa. Other people around do not get glimpse of such deep-rooted mental vices of the one's mind. Only one himself knows his mental vices. In general one's mind is full of uncalled vices resulting in sins, those have been accumulated with time in the mind. Such a mind can only be cleaned/ washed and made pure not merely by chanting the divine name merely through tongue/mouth, but by strong detergent / soap of divine name from the depth of his mind i.e. through Ajapa -Japa and getting completely dissolved in His glory. Dye of divine name that leads to mergence in the divinity with divine love and divine romance is the only means to remove such vices from mind. Furthermore, it also depends, how deep rooted are these vices. It may take a few days to a few months to years, may be complete life or may be couple of births. But mergence and to be one with the God's glory/name is the only means that is safest and unquestioned proven ways to dissolve/ remove the effect of vices from the mental frame.

The mergence in the divine name finally blesses the deep silence of mind of the devotee. In the fire of deep silence with no thoughts, all vices are washed away and nectar like purity develops in the mind. All divine qualities appear, perfection approaches in life of such a devotee. In fact such devotee gradually turns to be like semi God with full magnetic powers in his personality. He becomes capable of governing the life force, which acts according to his wish and evolve him by dissolving his past misdeeds/Karma.

It can never be analyzed/found out merely by seeing or being just in contact that one is sinner or divine personality.

Every body externally looks alike. It is not possible to distinguish the type of inner personality one posses. He may be greedy, with full of erotic thoughts, or egoistic or may be full of divinity. This will depend on the net past tendencies that are built in, because of his actions in the past life and in previous births. His net tendencies will indicate his past accumulated thoughts. He will think and act accordingly. In perfect conscious state, he visualizes his tendencies otherwise he is blindfolded and acts according to his built in thoughts and inclinations. His actions and way of living may be right or wrong. By taking shelter in the divinity and rigorously trying to uplift himself, he will be positively succeeded to overcome stored vices and become divine personality climbing the way to self-realization.

Guru Nanak Ji very clearly explains, as one will sow the same will he reaps. Every action in thoughts, words and deeds of an individual is recorded in a mysterious way by the norms laid out by Almighty. Every one gets fruits/ reaction of his action executed in any state of mind. By His order we come and go, take birth and die and again take birth. This is universal law of cause and effect, action and reaction. Vices executed by mind and done by physical actions, both will have effect. For mental vice, one gets mental harassment as the reaction of committed sins. For physical vices one gets capital punishment. Every action/karma, which is done by awareness/ presence of mind is getting recorded by divine laws, and has equal and opposite reaction. Laws of Almighty are same for every one. We out of our ignorance do not understand all this. By the command of Almighty one takes birth and leaves this world and this cycle goes on till one is self-realized and becomes Jeewan Mukta.

Equivalent Verses of Srimad Bhagavad Gita (Pauri 20)

Chapter 13

The Field And The Knower Of The Field

Three Approaches to Self-Realization (Verses 24-25)

ध्यानेनात्मनि पश्यन्ति केचिदात्मानमात्मना ।
अन्ये साङ्ख्येन योगेन कर्मयोगेन चापरे ॥२४॥

24. "While some perceive the Supreme Spirit in their heart by contemplation with their refined mind, some others know him by the yog of knowledge, and yet others by the yog of action."

अन्ये त्वेवमजानन्तः श्रुत्वान्येभ्य उपासते ।
तेऽपि चातितरन्त्येव मृत्युं श्रुतिपरायणाः ॥२५॥

25. "But ignorant of these ways, there are yet others who worship by just learning the truth from accomplished sages and, relying upon what they hear, they also doubtlessly steer across the gulf of the mortal world."

Pauri - 21

Teerath Tap Daiya Datt Dan

Je Ko Pavey Til Ka Maan

Suniya Maniya Man Kitta Bhau

Antargat Tirath Mal Nau

Sabh Gun Tere Mein Nahin Koye

Vin Gun Keete Bhagati Na Hoye

Suasat Aathi Bani Barmau

Sat Suhan Sada Man Chau

Kavan Su Vela Vakhat Kavan, Kavan Thit Kavan Vaar

Kavan Si Rut Maah Kavan Jit Hoya Akaar

Vel Na Paeeya Pandati Je Hove Lekh Puraan

Vakhat Na Paeeyo Kadian Je Likhan Lek Quraan

Thit Vaar Na Jogi Jane Rut Maah Na Koyee

Ja Karta Sirthi Ko Saje Aape Jane Soyee

Kiv Kar Aakhan Kiv Salaahi Kiyun Varni Kiv Jana

Nanak Aakhan Sabh Ko Akhey Ik Du Ik Siyana

Vadda Sahib Vaddi Naiyee Kitta Ja Ka Hovey

Nanak Je Ko Aape Jane Agge Gaya Na Sohey

Explanation

In this Pauri Guru Nanak Ji, explains the importance of self-improvement and cultivating the divine qualities within the self as compared to just following the path of performing rituals externally, and their futility.

It is really good of conducting the self by going to the places of pilgrimage to experience the divine vibrations. To donate, to have mercy on fellow beings, to do penance of different kinds by keeping fasts on various religious occasions etc. are indeed very good spiritual activities. This might give some individual satisfaction, some honor /glory one can earn in the society besides improving physical health by getting other divine blessings of the Almighty. But these are insignificant achievements in the spirituality. To achieve complete grace of Almighty in this life merely these external rituals are not adequate. For the Self –realization, devotees need recitation of divine Name, listening of divine glory, meditation on divine utterances, mergence in the deep meaning of knowledge / wisdom of His divine words. Furthermore, implementing and changing the life as per His command and execute all possible activities only for His service. One must cultivate all divine virtues i.e. contentment, foregiveness, love for fellow human beings etc and many more divine qualities in the internal frame of one's heart and mind. One must be merged in such qualities to be in divine love for Almighty. This will dissolve all the vices of the mind and one will turn to be pure. By taking bath in pilgrimage places, only physical cleaning is possible but by reciting divine name i.e. by Ajapa-japa, mind is rendered pure and vices get vanished, washed away on divine mergence. This is basically termed as internal divine bath.

Only mediation/mergence is the key as per Geeta and Japu Ji to become self radiant, pure and God-realized in this life it self. Starting from chanting/recitation of His name and then entering into Anahat Naad — the voiceless region, and gradually to the abode of silence and finally merging / expanding the self consciousness in the supreme consciousness and getting merge in that is the sole path of Self-realization.

Further highlighting the glory of Almighty, this Pauri depicts that all the existing virtues in this universe are personally His own divine virtues. No virtue belongs to a tiny creature created by Him. Unless and until, Almighty by His own Blessings doesn't create these divine virtues in a human being, it is not possible to become His devotee. He only picks and choose His devotees, generate His own virtues in the heart and convert Him as His favorite devotee. No one can be His devotee by one's own efforts and will. All these are greatness of Almighty that one sings and adore His glory, worship and merges in His divinity. He is the doer and He Himself is His own master. Truth, love, peace, contentment and work for Him without any selfish motives are a few of His virtues. By virtues only one can assess himself his own closeness with Almighty. Divine virtues are the divinity and divinity is God, the supreme light Himself. When divine virtues appeared in the created being then and then only there remains no difference between the created and the creator. Both created and creator, become the same. In other words God and His devotees become the same, and this is the devotion, the real grace and blessing of the creator on the created.

Almighty is ever glorious and omnipresent, omnipotent and changeless. Almighty is all in all. God Himself is delusion, the Maya. He Himself is Brahma, the Creator; He himself is divinity and divine words. Nothing is separate from Him. On one level Almighty is Maya and on the other level He is Brahma. There is no differentiation between His creation and in Him. He is present in every creation, takes care of the creation, and Himself takes formless form in each creation. Only the effect of Maya does not allow a creature to conceive this mysterious fact. How a body can survive without the force of Prana, which is the mysterious force of creation within us. Almighty is ever in Ananda, in joy. He is conscious, existence and Bliss. The union of this trinity is Brahma, He is ever true, in Bliss and in joy. We the created can become the same when the divinity is poured in our heart by the grace of Almighty, the supreme cosmic light.

In the continuation of this Pauri, Guru Nanak Ji explores the origin of the universe so as to express its magnamity. No power of the universe could express till to day, the time, the day, the date, the weather/season, month and year, when the Almighty has created this universe. Since all the creatures born after Almighty created the universe, so no one can ever know about its time of creation by God. Finite/creature is the part of infinite/creator so it is just not feasible by any norm to perceive about its origin and estimate the age of this mighty universe. Even learned scholars could not conceive the original period of holding and manifesting the creation of this universe by Almighty. Had they knew or could conceive about its origin, they might have succeeded to write a grand book like puranas on its appearance/origin. Even Mohammedan Moulavis and divine religious scholars, the Qaziz, did not have any concept of the creation of universe, otherwise they would have expressed their opinion and could have written many write-ups in the form of the big book on this subject like that of Koran/Quran.

Furthermore, it is said that great Indian Yogis by their rigorous penance could not visualize time, date, season, month etc. of the creation of this universe. No creature of this universe can express about this mystery. Creator of the universe only Himself knows when he has created this mighty universe. No one else can ever conceive its origin since all creatures appeared and evolved after million of years later after the universe was created.

Guru Nanak Ji says how the greatness of Almighty can be expressed, how His glory can be sung and by which means these can be discussed and adored and how small creatures like us can perceive this great timeless hidden mystery. All creatures want to express about this mystery of the Almighty by their own way considering as if each one of them is more wise and intelligent than the other. No creature understands that this mystery is mysterious mystery and is covered with infinite layers of complex mysteries. A finite creature can never conceive this mysterious origin.

Almighty and His power are immense. His greatness is beyond reach. Whatsoever is happening in this universe is as per His wish since He is the Originator and the Creator of the universe. Any creature, who tries to reach the source by his limited knowledge and wisdom, he can never reach the source and he will cease to receive any regard/honor from the Abode of Almighty. Even his progress may be curtailed by His command. In fact tiny creature created by infinite creator can never reach the depth of the concealed layers/wisdom of the Almighty. This universe is beyond time. Universe, which exists beyond time, is itself timeless. As Almighty is beyond time so the universe as created by Him. So neither one can know origin of Almighty and nor that of universe. Mergence in the glory of Almighty and that of universe is the only joy that a devotee must try to experience. One must meditate on the mysterious grand glory of Almighty. He only can reveal His mystery, and this is only possible as per His Wish only. He is the Master of the universe.

Equivalent Verses of Srimad Bhagavad Gita (Pauri 21)

Chapter 16

Embracing The Divine And Shunning The Demonic

The Soul Qualities That Make Man God-Like (Verses 1-3)

अभयं सत्त्वसंशुद्धिर्ज्ञानयोगव्यवस्थिति: ।
दानं दमश्च यज्ञश्च स्वाध्यायस्तप आर्जवम् ।।१।।

1. "The Lord said, 'Fearlessness, inner purity, steadfastness
of yog for knowledge, charity, continence, yagya, study of
scriptures, penance, and uprightness,...'"

अहिंसा सत्यमक्रोधस्त्याग: शान्तिरपैशुनम् ।
दया भूतेष्वलोलुप्त्वं मार्दवं ह्रीरचापलम् ।।२।।

2. "Nonviolence, truthfulness, abstinence of anger,
renunciation, tranquillity, absence of malice, compassion
for all beings, disinterestedness, tenderness, modesty,
abstinence from futile effort,..."

तेज: क्षमा धृति: शौचमद्रोहो नातिमानिता ।
भवन्ति सम्पदं दैवीमभिजातस्य भारत ।।३।।

3. "Magnificence, forgiveness, patience, purity of thought
and conduct, and absence of animosity and vanity-are (all)
attributes of the man endowed with divine riches."

Chapter 15

Purushottama: The Uttermost Being

The Supreme Spirit:

Beyond the Perishable and the Imperishable (Verses 16-20)

द्वाविमौ पुरुषौ लोके क्षरश्चाक्षर एव च।
क्षरः सर्वाणि भूतानि कूटस्थोऽक्षर उच्यते।।१६।।

16 "There are two kinds of beings in the world, the mortal and the immortal: whereas the bodies of all beings are destructible, their Souls are said to be imperishable."

उत्तमः पुरुषस्त्वन्यः परमात्मेत्युदाहृतः।
यो लोकत्रयमाविश्य बिभर्त्यव्यय ईश्वरः।।१७।।

17. "But higher than both of them is the one who pervades the three worlds to support and sustain all, and who is named the eternal God and Supreme Spirit (Ishwar)."

यस्मात्क्षरमतीतोऽहमक्षरादपि चोत्तमः।
अतोऽस्मि लोके वेदे च प्रथितः पुरुषोत्तमः।।१८।।

18. "Since I am supreme by virtue of being beyond both the perishable (body) and the imperishable (Soul), I am known as the Supreme Being (Purushottam) in the world as well as in the Ved."

यो मामेवमसम्मूढो जानाति पुरुषोत्तमम्।
स सर्वविद्भजति मां सर्वभावेन भारत।।१९।।

19. "The all-knowing man, who is thus aware of my essence, O Bharat, as the Supreme Being, always worships me with perfect devotion."

इति गुह्यतमं शास्त्रमिदमुक्तं मयानघ।
एतद्बुद्ध्वा बुद्धिमान्स्यात्कृतकृत्यश्च भारत।।२०।।

20. "I have thus instructed you, O the sinless, in this most subtle of all knowledge because, O Bharat, by knowing its essence a man gains wisdom and accomplishes all his tasks."

Pauri -22

Explanation

The infinite magnamity of the vast universe has been expressed in words, however its description is beyond words and any counts. In the vast Universe, there are countess nether regions one below the other. Also there are countless heavens one above the other. From generation people are tired of searching the frontier of Creation. Finally, Vedas proclaimed this conclusion that expanse of the formed Universe by Almighty is endless. Beyond saying and using words like countless and endless, nothing more could be added. Even modern science after the long research of centuries could arrive at this conclusion that Creation has no boundaries and it is only expanding every moment. It is infinite. Even to use the word "infinite" is too meager for the limitless magnamity of the ever-expanding Universe.

Furthermore, it is written/said in many books of Islam and Christianity that even eighteen thousand Universes do exist but the main omnipresent power behind the formation of countless Universes is the same, which is changeless, omnipotent and omniscient. There is no account of any form, shape and type, otherwise these could have been properly recorded by the great ancient scholars and Self -realized personalities, born and existed in this world. To write about Him, one may try, but while writing about infinity, one will only die, lifetime is not adequate to express iota of His glory. In fact, it is beyond expression and within the capacity of being written by words and counts. It is very evident in other words that the Creation of Almighty cannot be greater than Him that could count its expanse and magnamity. Ultimately, the essence, which Guru Nanak Dev Ji says is that He is the greatest of the greatest and He Himself knows His greatness. It is as if others are showing lamp to the shining sun by counting His wonders and glories in the Universe.

The inner meaning of this Pauri may be depicted that in our Chidakasa, there is so much expanse of His mysteries that one can never be exhausted probing these and merging in these wonders of Almighty in the stage of deep meditation. Our Chidakasa is like the magnificent manifested Universe with all divine wisdom, knowledge, and can only be perceived by intuition in the state of deep silence by the grace of Almighty. This goes on expanding as one goes in the deep depth of meditation on Self. Every moment it gives the fresh joy and virtues. As in the physical universe, one can discover the similar pattern of heaven skies and nether regions with unending depth and inexpressible glory in the region of Chidakasa region of his head below the apex center/Sahasara under the vicinity of the tenth gate. Basically within each one of us is the presence of divine power, the Creator, the Infinite, in the miniature way as it exists in the outward universe. One can visualizes this mystery in the deep state of Savikalpa Samadhi. The same is highlighted in Vedas. But coming out from this state one is unable to express these wonders. There are no words to describe. That is the reason all knowledge is within us and it comes out gradually as the perfection in Self —realization manifested/expanded with time in deep meditation. God has created universe in each one of His creature and as He is omnipresent externally so He in present internally in all His creations. Only manifestation of divine qualities is needed for His expression from within us to the external world. This is the secret of scientific progress, which is generated within and gradually takes the form of physical expression. All knowledge is His. By human evolution, wisdom is expanded and is appeared in various forms in the external world.

In short, His greatness and mystery, He only knows. We must try to merge in Him and every aspects of His mystery gradually will be enlightened by it self by His grace and Blessings.

Equivalent Verses of Srimad Bhagavad Gita (Pauri 22)

Chapter 7

The Nature Of Spirit And The Spirit Of Nature

How the Creator Sustains the Manifested Creation (Verses 7-9)

मत्तः परतरं नान्यत्किञ्चिदस्ति धनञ्जय।
मयि सर्वमिदं प्रोतं सूत्रे मणिगणा इव॥७॥

7. "There is, O Dhananjay, not even one object other than me, and the whole world is linked up with me like the pearls of a necklace."

रसोऽहमप्सु कौन्तेय प्रभास्मि शशिसूर्ययोः।
प्रणवः सर्ववेदेषु शब्दः खे पौरुषं नृषु॥८॥

8. "O Arjun, I am that which makes water liquescent, the radiance in the sun and the moon, the sacred syllable OM, the word's echo (Shabd) in the ether, and I am also the manliness in men."

पुण्यो गन्धः पृथिव्यां च तेजश्चास्मि विभावसौ।
जीवनं सर्वभूतेषु तपश्चास्मि तपस्विषु॥९॥

9. "I am the fragrance in the earth, the flame in fire, the Soul that animates all beings, and the penance of ascetics."

Pauri - 23

Explanation

In this Pauri, the importance of the mystery of mergence in the vast expanse and manifestation of the Almighty has been explicitly brought out. Pauri depicts that Almighty is greatest of the greatest in all respects. People worship Him. Praise and adoration is commonly done for Him since creatures formed by Him know that only by His blessings and grace, one can live and survive. With all this, no body is able to conceive the greatest mystery of the Almighty, the Cosmic supreme power. People generally talk, discuss and sing His glory in all possible way to adore Him. But no body could recognize and reveal His infinite glory with all such prayers and adorations. Even people forget themselves by such adorations but could not succeed to identify and recognize Him.

It is similar to the situation of various rivers and canals those finally get merge after crossing planes and fields into the ocean, but never find the limitless boundaries of the ocean even after mergence. To know the magnamity of the ocean, rivers must be large and bigger than ocean, which is not feasible. A finite cannot observe infinite. It has to be bigger than infinite to recognize it, and it is not practicable for a finite. This makes very vivid that it is impossible to know Almighty, but it is possible to get absorb in Him, to take dip in its divinity, to get merge in Him and take joy of the mergence. His knowledge is beyond one's absorption but it is feasible to merge in His supreme light of wisdom and knowledge. So, by devotion, one can merge in Him, enjoy the glory of His presence and by devotion and love, one can joy and have taste of His wonderful and mysterious beauty.

In fact He is far beyond words/speech and mind of a human being. Mind and human wisdom cannot approach to His vicinity. Devotion and Love for Him are the means and perfect suitable ladder to climb to get merge in the infinite source. He reveals Himself to His devotees by the pure language of devotion and devotion is beyond material, and costs nothing. Devotion and love for Him is by His grace only, and one cannot have abstract love without for any one without form and shape. God devotion is feasible when one really become indifferent from this material world and understands/perceives from the bottom of the heart his transient/temporary existence on this earth, and when one seizes to extract any happiness from any of the worldly sources.

The kingdom of a great emperor is considered really very great, which has under his control the large territory of the resources of ocean since ocean has treasure of very important materials in its deep depth, which just needs to be exploited. Besides the control on ocean, if kingdom has plenty of land and mountains of richness, it is really a very splendid kingdom, and emperor of such a kingdom is beyond imagination of richness and command high regards all around. But even such a king does not get any regard in the kingdom of God. The king's prestige in the kingdom of Almighty is considered even lower than that of a smallest ant, which always remembers the glory of the Almighty.

In the nutshell this Pauri conveys the importance of the glory of the remberance of Almighty in the background of one's mind and brings out very vividly the importance of the mergence of devotee in the glory of Almighty in comparison to trying to conceive and know His mystery of existence. To taste the joy of mergence in His glory is wonderful and one must concentrate his efforts with great devotion to merge in it by meditation and listening the voiceless voice of Almighty. In short, an emperor with treasurers and dominion equal to vast like the Ocean is not equal to an ant, whose heart retains the Love of God.

Equivalent Verses of Srimad Bhagavad Gita (Pauri 23)

Chapter 18

In Truth Do I Promise Thee: Thou Shalt Attain Me

Summary of the Gita's Message: How God-Realization is Attained (Verses 56)

सर्वकर्माण्यपि सदा कुर्वाणो मद्व्यपाश्रयः ।
मत्प्रसादादवाप्नोति शाश्वतं पदमव्ययम् ॥५६॥

56. "Although engaged in action whole heartedly, one who finds refuge in me achieves the everlasting, indestructible, final bliss."

Pauri - 24

Ant Na Siphti Kahen Na Ant

Ant Na Karne Dein Na Ant

Ant Na Vekhan Sunan Na Ant

Ant Na Japey Kya Man Mant

Ant Na Japey Keeta Aakar

Ant Na Japey Paravaar

Ant Karan Kete Billahe

Ta Ke Ant Na Paye Jahe

Ehu Ant Na Janne Koye

Bahuta Kahiye Bahuta Hoye

Vadda Sahib Uncha Thaun

Unche Ooper Unchan Naun

Evad Uncha Hove Koye

Tis Unche Ko Janne Soye

Jevad Aap Janne Aap Aap

Nanak Nadri Karmi Daat

Explanation

The Pauri in general depicts that virtues of the God is beyond comprehension. In the same way inner divine virtues of the man of Self-realization are limitless.

Qualities/praises of Almighty are countless. His virtues/ glories are infinite and beyond expressions and the countable numbers. There is no end of His Creation, and His Blessings, Gifts and Grace on His Creations are beyond comprehension. Even just by observing and listening, one cannot comprehend His boundless qualities of Creation and virtues of His nature. It is not possible what the Almighty has stored within Himself for the welfare of His Creation/universe. His limitless sight and endless listening and infinite mental capabilities are not within comprehension. His direction and approach are mysterious. One/the finite cannot approach the depth of Almighty/infinite to visualize/conceive the mystery stored in the core of timeless and omnipresent Almighty. Unfathomable is the extent of His creation and Unknowable is the boundary of Almighty for an individual. It is impossible to conceive the horizon of His Creation. Width and depth of His endless creation cannot be imagined.

People have been trying from generations to estimate the boundary and expanse of His Creation, but so far no one could succeed to disclose this mystery and even move an iota in this direction. All those, who tried and vexed to know Him, were disgusted/disappointed but could not get an end of Him. His endless glory cannot be listed. More and more if one puts his efforts in this direction to probe the greatness of His glory, His glory goes on increasing multifold. His greatness is expanding as one tries to be close to the virtues of His glories. His creation is expanding every moment. In other words, as one manifests his imagination about the virtues of Almighty, He seems to expand His virtues, and the finite creature finds himself more away and away from his imagination/concept of Almighty. More one describes Him, much more he is found to be unfound. God's/His existence is the unidentified mysterious mystery of the Cosmos since He Himself is the supreme Cosmic Light.

Almighty is Him self the greatest and His position is supreme. His name is still on much higher platform in comparison to His position. He is exalted but higher than Him is His exalted name. Status of His name in His glory is much higher than the status of Almighty. It is clear that by reciting the name of Almighty and getting merge in the name of His glory, the status of devotee is uplifted and He becomes as perfect as God in divine virtues. Under these conditions there remains no difference between God and His devotee. Both become the same and merge in each other. Furthermore love for Almighty is on the highest plane than that of His name and formless form of Almighty. Intrinsic love of devotee towards God places him on the highest pedestal of spirituality and nothing is greater than this position in His creation. Any one, who is really on higher position than Him, can visualize the greatness of Almighty, and importance of love and intrinsic value of a devotee and the divine virtues cultivated in devotee by Him. Since no one is greater than Almighty, so only He knows His own greatness and supremacy. In essence, His majesty only He alone knows.

Guru Nanak Ji says that by the blessings of Almighty, one gets divine gift of His name i.e. chanting of His glory, which raises the devotee to much higher level than the Almighty Himself. By one's own efforts, there is insignificant gain, however what one really achieves is what Almighty desires. Without His Will, one gets no knowledge, no gains and no achievements in life. With one's own intelligence, no divine knowledge can be cultivated. The knowledge to an individual is by His grace and it is a divine gift. In fact, by His Grace and Bounty is what one may know.

The intrinsic meaning of this Pauri is full of mystery. It means that the man of Self –realization, who is merged in divine glory develops limitless divinity and divine virtues virtues. He develops the miraculous power of visualization by his developed intuition. His mental capabilities are enhanced. His imagination has no boundaries. It is difficult to estimate his capabilities and inner development. His developed capabilities really surprise others. Only other self realized souls could understand him. For an ordinary human being his actions and inbuilt divine capabilities are full of mystery. Still he considers himself with humility and no egoism is seen in him. From heart to heart, he only knows it is divine grace and divine powers, which have developed in him by virtue of mergence in divine glory in deep meditation as a result of Self-realization by His grace. He is intrinsically clear that grace of Almighty is operating through him, and it is His blessing only.

Equivalent Verses of Srimad Bhagavad Gita (Pauri 24)

Chapter 11

Vision Of Visions, The Lord Reveals His Cosmic Form (Verses 1-15)

अर्जुन उवाच
मदनुग्रहाय परमं गुह्यमध्यात्मसञ्ज्ञितम् ।
यत्त्वयोक्तं वचस्तेन मोहोऽयं विगतो मम ।।१।।

1. "Arjun said, 'The compassionate words with which you have instructed me in the secret and most exalted knowledge have dispelled my ignorance.'"

भवाप्ययौ हि भूतानां श्रुतौ विस्तरशो मया ।
त्वत्तः कमलपत्राक्ष माहात्म्यमपि चाव्ययम् ।।२।।

2. "For I have learnt from you, O the lotus-eyed, not only a detailed account of the origin and dissolution of beings, but also of your imperishable glory."

एवमेतद्यथात्थ त्वमात्मानं परमेश्वर ।
द्रष्टुमिच्छामि ते रूपमैश्वरं पुरुषोत्तम ।।३।।

3. "You are, O Lord, what you have told me, but I wish, O Supreme Being, to have a direct vision of your form in all its divine magnificence."

मन्यसे यदि तच्छक्यं मया द्रष्टुमिति प्रभो ।
योगेश्वर ततो मे त्वं दर्शयात्मानमव्ययम् ।।४।।

4."Show me, O Lord, your eternal form if you consider,O Yogeshwar, that it is possible to see it."

पश्य मे पार्थ रूपाणि शतशोऽथ सहस्रशः।
नानाविधानि दिव्यानि नानावर्णाकृतीनि च॥५॥

5. "The Lord said, 'Behold, O Parth, my hundreds and thousands of various celestial manifestations of different hues and forms.'"

पश्यादित्यान्वसून्रुद्रानश्विनौ मरुत्तस्तथा।
बहून्यदृष्टपूर्वाणि पश्याश्चर्याणि भारत॥६॥

6. "See in me, O Bharat, the sons of Aditi, the Rudr, the Vasu, the Ashwin brothers, and the Marut, as well as numerous other marvellous forms that have not been seen before."

इहैकस्थं जगत्कृत्स्नं पश्याद्य सचराचरम्।
मम देहे गुडाकेश यच्चान्यद्द्रष्टुमिच्छसि॥७॥

7. 'Now, O Gudakesh, see in my body at this one place the whole animate and inanimate world, and whatever else you desire to know."

न तु मां शक्यसे द्रष्टुमनेनैव स्वचक्षुषा।
दिव्यं ददामि ते चक्षुः पश्य मे योगमैश्वरम्॥८॥

8. "But since you cannot see me with your physical eyes, I grant you divine vision with which you may behold my magnificence and the might of my yog."

एवमुक्त्वा ततो राजन्महायोगेश्वरो हरिः।
दर्शयामास पार्थाय परमं रूपमैश्वरम्॥९॥

9. "Sanjay said (to Dhritrashtr), 'After speaking thus, O King, the Lord-the great master of yog-revealed his supreme, omnipresent form to Arjun.'"

अनेकवक्त्रनयनमनेकाद्भुतदर्शनम् ।
अनेकदिव्याभरणं दिव्यानेकोद्यतायुधम् ॥१०॥
दिव्यमाल्याम्बरधरं दिव्यगन्धानुलेपनम् ।
सर्वाश्चर्यमयं देवमनन्तं विश्वतोमुखम् ॥११॥

10-11. "And (Arjun beheld before himself) the infinite, all-pervading God with numerous mouths and eyes, many wondrous manifestations, decked with various ornaments, carrying many weapons in his hands, wearing celestial garlands and apparel, anointed with heavenly perfumes, and endowed with all kinds of wonder."

दिवि सूर्यसहस्रस्य भवेद्युगपदुत्थिता ।
यदि भाः सदृशी सा स्याद्भासस्तस्य महात्मनः ॥१२॥

12. "Even the light of a thousand suns in the sky could hardly match the radiance of the omnipresent God."

तत्रैकस्थं जगत्कृत्स्नं प्रविभक्तमनेकधा ।
अपश्यद्देवदेवस्य शरीरे पाण्डवस्तदा ॥१३॥

13. "Pandu's son (Arjun) then saw in the body of Krishn, the God of gods, the many separate worlds together.

ततः स विस्मयाविष्टो हृष्टरोमा धनञ्जयः ।
प्रणम्य शिरसा देवं कृताञ्जलिरभाषत ॥१४॥

14. "Then overwhelmed by awe and with his hair standing on end, Arjun paid obeisance to the great God and spoke thus with folded hands."

पश्यामि देवांस्तव देव देहे सर्वांस्तथा भूतविशेषसङ्घान् ।
ब्रह्माणमीशं कमलासनस्थ-मृषींश्च सर्वानुरगांश्च दिव्यान् ।।१५।।

15. "Arjun said, 'I see in you, O Lord, all the gods, hosts of
beings. Brahma on his lotus-seat, Mahadev, all the great
sages, and miraculous serpents.'"

Pauri - 25

Bahuta Karam Likhia Na Jaye

Vada Data Til Na Tamaye

Kete Mangeh Jodh Apaar

Ketian Ganat Nahin Vichaar

Kete Khap Tutte Vekar

Kete Lai Lai Mukkar Pahin

Kete Moorakh Khahi Khahin

Ketian Dookh Bhookh Sud Mar

Ehi Bhi Daat Teri Dataar

Bund Khalasi Bhane Hoye

Hore Akh Na Sakkey Koye

Je Ko Khaik Akhan Payee

Ohu Janey Jetian Muhin Khayee

Aape Jane Aape Deyee

Akhain Si Bhi Keti Keyee

Jis Nu Bakshe Siphat Salaah

Nanak Patisahi Patisahu

Explanation

There is no way to measure His splendid glory. His gifts and Blessings are immense and His abundant glories are not feasible to record. He is selfless. His benevolence has no iota of greed. He is greatest selfless donor and does not expect any return from any creature after donating. No one is capable of returning His gifts/ donations since all are created by Him, and belong to Him only. An individual is just a Custodian to preserve His reserves and uses what He gives. Even if some one donates Him, he must understand that nothing belongs to an individual, he is donating back to Almighty what He has gifted. He is the owner and master of one and all. He gives without any desire of return by any form and means. He desires only divine love from His devotees and Almighty knows that only love belongs personally to the devotees and it is the highest offer, which they can offer to Almighty in return to His benevolence.

There are countless warriors, brave personalities of world and many valiant, who beg and look for various blessings from His divine door. Spiritual people only beg for divine grace and they don't beg for material goods from Him. A devotee and spiritually uplifted only beg for God, His virtues, divine values and nothing more from Him. Number of beggars is infinite in the universe and cannot be imagined since almost all His creatures only beg for the worldly comforts and they have long list of begging. Hardly any one really begs divine qualities to become like Him. There are many such beggars on His door, those after fulfilling their worldly desires from His grace, get themselves trapped in different earthly vices and finally completely ruin themselves. They are trapped in sensual pleasures beyond limitation and loss all worldly comforts and return back to square one having nothing left in their disposal. They did not appreciate and value of the blessings of Almighty under the influence of vices.

There are many such people who are never obliged by the various comforts allocated by Almignty to them. They enjoy all the gifts given by the God and never even think to thank Him for all such priceless blessings gifted by Him, which he is enjoying every moment. Some don't acknowledge after receiving His blessings and grace. They negate what they receive. They just forget Him after their desires are fulfilled. There are many fools those who are obsessed with greed and go on eating and enjoying all comforts but never acknowledges the presence of Almighty, the Universal donor of every comfort to them.

There is another class of creation in this universe who always suffer because of hunger and various other physical and mental pains, but they consider all such sufferings are as per the Will of Almighty, and reactions of their past evil actions. Many such people who are afflicted with pain, they consider this entire as divine plan, and they accept all such suffering with joy considering them as the blessings of Almighty. They perceive that these sufferings are from the highest source of Almighty, to make them understand to live as per His Wish as per the law of cause and effect, action and reaction. They are blessed with divine wisdom, which make them understand that these sufferings are to develop dissipation in their heart so that they get further attached with the name and Japa of Almighty and get merge in Him, the timeless identity. They always consider that Almighty is honoring them with His divine grace. They know fully well that gold can only be purified when it passes through fire. Vices can only be shed/washed when the devotees bear/take the pain of worldly sufferings with joy. This is the divine law.

His affectionate devotees admit that liberation from bondage of repeated series of birth and death is only by the Wish, gift and blessings of Almighty. So they believe to live under the shelter of His Wish. They completely surrender to His Wish. They take joy, happiness and sufferings identically in the same pattern as the gift from Almighty without any complain and inhibition of any kind to Him. No body on earth can suggest any other alternative means to live for liberation from bondage of births and death except to follow the Wish of divinity, the Almighty. Only fools out of total ignorance suggest the alternative means for liberation and they don't know that only disgrace will come on their way in their life span. There is no other ladder to climb except that of blessing of Almighty, His grace and to live as per His command, completely surrendering to Him by thoughts, words and deeds. Except devotion, love and mergence in His glory, other paths lead to darkness of hell and not to the doorstep of liberation. Only sufferer will know the consequences of following the alternative path that goes against the laws of divinity.

Almighty knows the needs of devotees, and He satisfies their needs. A very few uplifted devotees experience this divine grace of Cosmic power, which is omniscient. Self-realized devotees very clearly conceive that intuition is developed by His grace as if He /Almighty has occupied the seat in their heart and operates by His own Will. Almighty is infinite. He is beyond of beyond. Almighty Himself by His own grace enlightens the devotee to magnify His glories, to sing and immerge in His glories of absolute silence.

Guru Nanak Ji says that Almighty, the Supernal graces His devotee Himself and uplift him to the level of emperor of emperors i.e. to the level equivalent to Himself. Surely, His divine grace bestows the devotees to the level of the king of kings.

Inner meaning of this Pauri clearly depicts that after the enlightenment on achieving the Self-realization, the blessing endowed on the devotee is immense. He becomes self less, the biggest donor, the liberated, Jeewan Mukta, and the king of kings in his life. On the contrary, if one is trapped in vices, he becomes selfish, foolish and suffers throughout his life and gets trapped in the cycles of rebirths. Indeed one must follow the path of divinity to uplift him by achieving silence on passing through the thoughtless state by the grace of Almighty.

Equivalent Verses of Srimad Bhagavad Gita (Pauri 25)

Chapter 9

The Royal Knowledge, The Royal Mystery

How the Lord Pervades all Creation, Yet remains Transcendent (Verses 4-11)

मया ततमिदं सर्वं जगदव्यक्तमूर्तिना।
मत्स्थानि सर्वभूतानि न चाहं तेष्ववस्थितः।।४।।

4. "The whole world is pervaded by me, the unmanifest Supreme Being, and all beings dwell within my will but I am not in them."

न च मत्स्थानि भूतानि पश्य मे योगमैश्वरम्।
भूतभृन्न च भूतस्थो ममात्मा भूतभावनः।।५।।

5. "And even all beings are not within me, and such is the power of my yog-maya that my Spirit, the creator and preserver of all beings, is not within them."

यथाकाशस्थितो नित्यं वायुः सर्वत्रगो महान्।
तथा सर्वाणि भूतानि मत्स्थानीत्युपधारय।।६।।

6. "Be it known to you that all beings dwell in me just as the great wind that roams everywhere always dwells in the sky."

सर्वभूतानि कौन्तेय प्रकृतिं यान्ति मामिकाम्।
कल्पक्षये पुनस्तानि कल्पादौ विसृजाम्यहम्।।७।।

7. "All beings, O son of Kunti, attain to my nature and merge into it at the end of a cycle (kalp) and I recreate them at the beginning of another cycle."

प्रकृतिं स्वामवष्टभ्य विसृजामि पुनः पुनः।
भूतग्राममिमं कृत्स्नमवशं प्रकृतेर्वशात्।।८।।

8. "I repeatedly shape all these beings, who are helplessly dependent on their innate properties, according to their action."

न च मां तानि कर्माणि निबध्नन्ति धनञ्जय।
उदासीनवदासीनमसक्तं तेषु कर्मसु।।९।।

9. "Unattached and disinterested in these acts, O Dhananjay, I am not bound by action."

मयाध्यक्षेण प्रकृतिः सूयते सचराचरम्।
हेतुनानेन कौन्तेय जगद्विपरिवर्तते।।१०।।

10. "In association with me, O son of Kunti, my maya shapes this world of the animate and the inanimate , and the world revolves like a wheel of recurrence for the aforesaid reason."

अवजानन्ति मां मूढा मानुषीं तनुमाश्रितम्।
परं भावमजानन्तो मम भूतमहेश्वरम्।।११।।

11. "The deluded who do not know my ultimate being regard me in the human form as but an inferior mortal."

Pauri - 26

Amul Gun Amul Vapar
Amul Vapariye Amul Bhandar
Amul Aaveh Amul Lai Jahin
Amul Bhayee Amula Samahi
Amul Dharam Amul Dibaan
Amul Tul Amul Parvan
Amul Bakhsis Amul Nisan
Amul Karam Amul Phurman
Amulon Amul Aakhia Na Jayee
Akh Akh Rahe Liv Layee
Akhain Ved Path Puraan
Akhain Pare Karhi Vakhiyan
Akhain Barme Akhain Ind
Akhain Gopi Te Govind
Akhain Isar Akhain Sidh
Akhain Kete Keete Budh
Akhain Danav Akhain Dev
Akhain Sur Nar Muni Jan Sev
Kete Akhain Akhan Pahi
Kete Kahi Kahi Uth Uth Jahi
Ete Keete Hore Karehi
Tan akh na sakke kei kei
Jevad Bhave Tevad Hoye
Nanak Janne Sacha Soye
Je Ko Akhai Bol Vigaar
Tan Likhiye Sir Gavaran Gavaru

Explanation

In this Pauri priceless attribute, priceless dispensation of Almighty, and His immense importance in different aspects are expressed. Any activity, taken up with the priceless attributes of God, is in deed a priceless activity. Such divine activity is only for the welfare of humanity and it is a selfless service to the mankind. Such activities are pure to the extend possible, and these are by Him, by His devotees, and for Him only. Such activities are flourished and priceless wealth is earned for the welfare of society. Furthermore, a person engaged in such an activity, is immersed in divinity, and work for Almighty, becomes priceless jewel for human being with time. By this process, he cultivates only divine virtues. His quality of life is enhanced and his priceless virtues are stored up within him besides expanse of worldly goods through his divinity, honest and fare actions. Such dealer/divine worker in fact increases the wealth of virtuous treasures in his Samaskaras since all his activities revolve only around divinity.

They/such people are really blessed with divine grace that increases both their divine wealth and worldly wealth. They become like Him. Great saints of the world, who spread His name and fame, are not less than Him. They are worshiped at par with Almighty. All such people are great who are engaged in working for spreading His glory, and also who interact with such divotees and offer them attributes. They do get the love of God as the raw white cloth get the same color in which it is immerged. In the nutshell, any one whosoever is involved in divine activity, whether he is devotee, scholar, spiritual aspirant or who is completely merged in divinity, are priceless in all respects. No one can pay the price of their virtues, they posses. All those, who love the divine glories of Almighty and those immerged in love for Him, are priceless unique personalities of this world.

The divine religion and its laws/regulations are priceless and all such places/courts where divine virtues and supernal qualities are weighted and discussed are superior and priceless. To follow these laws and live according to such regulations is extremely difficult task. There is no comparison of such a divine personality with any one whose thoughts; words and deeds are as per divinity. No one can price/buy such a devotee by his wealth. He is beyond wealth. By wealth, no body can accumulate divine qualities and change his way of living accordingly. Moreover, priceless are the laws and means of divine judgment. The divine judgment is made not based on merely the external physical involvement in the activity by any one. The motives, purity of heart and intentions of an individual are divine balances used to weigh, the fruits/outcome of the executed actions. Divine weights used by Almighty to measure real value of the activities are mysterious, and concepts of these weights/activities are beyond the human apprehension. Whether the human mind is concentrated completely/partially with the activities being executed, all these are assessed by the mysterious norms of the Lord to grant His priceless blessings to the executer. By any social norms/means, divine judgments are not executed. Blessings of Almighty and His recognition for human efforts, unique and mysterious commands used by him, cannot be imagined. His overall assessment for an individual, for the reactions of one's action to grant him fruits/punishment are all beyond and beyond of human mind. His way of approach and gifts are priceless. His forgiveness for one's sins and rewards for good actions are as per His priceless commands. His decisions, He implements as He Wishes and no power can go against His decisions. He is fearless, selfless and His approach is priceless to uplift human being to take them to the path of spirituality. In short, His laws of the divine court and flawless scales used for graceful judgment render priceless blessings with His defined mark thereon.

All aspects of the divine force are priceless, beyond human expressions & assumptions. Words cannot be used beyond limits to express His magnamity. All words and expression lose their power since His glory is beyond of beyond expressions. Finally each one after exhausting all resources of their expressions, become silent. He feels to enter in the abode of silence since no more way is left to express glory of Almighty. Only in silence state, crossing thoughtless regime, on entering the state of Samadhi, on merging with Him, one could get/taste the nectar of His glory, which is beyond expression by any means.

All Vedas, Vedic hymns, Puranas and scriptures try to dwell on the glories of Almighty, learned scholars converse about His virtues and qualities to the extend possible. All demy gods including Brahma, Indra, Goppies/Maidens, Govind/Krishna and other uplifted divine souls dwell His glories by different ways/ means, but never succeeded to accomplish to fulfill to the required extend. Lord Shiva, Shivaites and other accomplished great souls, many Buddha, divine personalities, demons, deities, dummy Gods, sages, saints and men devoted to divine services of all religions including Buddhism, Jainism shavism bow to His glory, adore Him and have been constantly engaged to dwell the divine glory, but never succeeded.

There are many still expressing the divine glories and many more are constantly trying by various means. There are many after trying and trying to express the divine glory, have left this world to their journey abode. Still generation after generation, people take birth by His grace, and are continued expressing His endless glories. How long this process will continue generation after generation, is beyond the purview of any description. Still the expression of limitless glories of the omnipotent Almighty will never be completed. This is because of the fact that the Almighty is infinite and He Himself expands further as per His Wish. So, one in any generation and in generations to come can never accomplish the expressions of invaluable manifestation of His glories. If Almighty was to create continuously many more human beings/creatures in this universe, yet He will remain inexpressible and as wondrous to all of them as pleases Him.

Guru Nanak Ji says He can become as great as He wishes. Thy greatness is only known to Thee only. He is beyond time and ever new. He is not affected by time. He Himself knows His form and shape. His manifestation is entirely under His own control. If anyone claims that God can be described then he must be declared not only as stupid among fools, but the king of fools.

The inner inexpressible meaning of this Pauri is that after self- realization, the devotee cultivates priceless divine virtues. He becomes undoubtedly pure in all his dealings. He is blessed by God's grace in all aspects. The description of his perception and wisdom is beyond the reach of learned scholars. Everyone praises him because of his purity of heart and selfless services. His list of mysterious qualities is beyond description. In short, the divinity developed in a common human being turn him to be superior in all respect. He becomes perfect with time.

Equivalent Verses of Srimad Bhagavad Gita (Pauri 26)

Chapter 9

The Royal Knowledge, The Royal Mystery

How the Lord Pervades all Creation, Yet remains Transcendent (Verses 16-19)

अहं क्रतुरहं यज्ञः स्वधाहमहमौषधम्।
मन्त्रोऽहमहमेवाज्यमहमग्निरहं हुतम्।।१६।।

16. "I am the action that is undertaken, the yagya, the fulfillment of earlier resolutions, the healer, the sacred prayer, the oblation as well as the sacred fire, and I am also the sacrificial act of oblation."

पिताहमस्य जगतो माता धाता पितामहः।
वेद्यं पवित्रमोङ्कार ऋक्साम यजुरेव च।।१७।।

17. "And I too am the bearer and preserver of the whole world as also the giver of rewards for action; father, mother and also the grandsire; the sacred, imperishable OM who is worthy of being known; and all Ved-Rig, Sam and Yajur."

गतिर्भर्ता प्रभुः साक्षी निवासः शरणं सुहृत्।
प्रभवः प्रलयः स्थानं निधानं बीजमव्ययम्।।१८।।

18. "I am the supreme goal, the sustainer and Lord of all, the maker of good and evil, the abode and shelter of all, the benefactor who wants nothing in return, the beginning and the end, the fountainhead as well as that in whom all beings are dissolved, and also the indestructible primal energy."

तपाम्यहमहं वर्षं निगृह्णाम्युत्सृजामि च।
अमृतं चैव मृत्युश्च सदसच्चाहमर्जुन ।।१९।।

19. "I am the sun that burns, I draw the clouds and also make them rain, and, O Arjun, I am the drought of immortality as well as death, and I am also both substance and shadow."

The Right Method of Worshiping God (Verses 20-26)

त्रैविद्या मां सोमपाः पूतपापा यज्ञैरिष्ट्वा स्वर्गति प्रार्थयन्ते।
ते पुण्यमासाद्य सुरेन्द्रलोक-मश्नन्ति दिव्यान्दिवि देवभोगान् ।।२०।।

20. "Men who do pious deeds enjoined by the three Ved, who have tasted nectar and freed themselves from sin, and who wish for heavenly existence through worshipping me by yagya, go to heaven (Indrlok) and enjoy godly pleasures as a reward for their virtuous acts."

ते तं भुक्त्वा स्वर्गलोकं विशालं क्षीणे पुण्ये मर्त्यलोकं विशन्ति।
एवं त्रयीधर्ममनुप्रपन्ना गतागतं कामकामा लभन्ते ।।२१।।

21 "With the gradual wearing out of the merits of their piety, they go back to the mortal world after enjoying the pleasures of great heaven ; and it is thus that they who seek refuge in the desire-oriented action prescribed by the three Ved and covet joy are condemned to repeated death and birth."

अनन्याश्चिन्तयन्तो मां ये जनाः पर्युपासते।
तेषां नित्याभियुक्तानां योगक्षेमं वहाम्यहम् ।।२२।।

22. "I myself protect the yog of men who abide in me with steady and undeviating faith and who worship me selflessly, constantly remembering me as God."

येऽप्यन्यदेवता भक्ता यजन्ते श्रद्धयान्विताः।
तेऽपि मामेव कौन्तेय यजन्त्यविधिपूर्वकम्।।२३।।

23. "Although even covetous devotees indeed worship me in worshipping other gods, their worship is against the ordained provision and therefore enveloped by ignorance."

अहं हि सर्वयज्ञानां भोक्ता च प्रभुरेव च।
न तु मामभिजानन्ति तत्त्वेनातश्च्यवन्ति ते।।२४।।

24. 'They have to go undergo rebirth because they are ignorant of the reality that I am the enjoyer as well as the master of all yagya."

यान्ति देवव्रता देवान्पितृन्यान्ति पितृव्रताः।
भूतानि यान्ति भूतेज्या यान्ति मद्याजिनोऽपि माम्।।२५।।

25. "Men who are devoted to gods attain to gods, worshippers of ancestors attain to their ancestors, worshippers of beings attain to the state of beings, and my worshippers attain to me."

पत्रं पुष्पं फलं तोयं यो मे भक्त्या प्रयच्छति।
तदहं भक्त्युपहृतमश्नामि प्रयतात्मनः।।२६।।

26. 'I lovingly accept the offerings of leaves, flowers, fruit, and water the selfless worshipper makes to me with true devotion."

Pauri - 27

So Dar Keha So Ghar Keha Jit Bah Sarab Sambhale

Vaje Nad Anek Sankha Kete Vavanhare

Kete Raag Pari Siun Kahian Kete Gavanhare

Gavahi Tuhno Paun Pani Baisantar Gave Raja Dharam Duare

Gavahi Chit Gupt Likh Janahi Likh Likh Dharam Vichare

Gavahi Isar Barma Devi Sohan Sada Savare

Gavahi Ind Indasan Baithe Devatian Dar Nale

Gavahi Siddh Samadhi Andar Gavan Sadh Vichare

Gavan Jatti Sati Santokhi Gavahi Veer Karare

Gavan Pandit Paran Rakhisar Jug Jug Vedan Nale

Gavahi Mohania Man Mohani Surga Machh Paiyale

Gavan Ratan Upaye Tere Athsath Teerath Nale

Gavahi Jodh Mahabal Sura Gavahi Khani Chare

Gavahi Khand Mandal Varbhanda Kar Kar Rakhe Dhare

Sei Tudh Nu Gavan Jo Tudh Bhavan Ratte Tere Bhagat Rasale

Hor Kete Gavan Se Mein Chitt Na Avan Nanak Kiya Vichare

Soi Soi Sada Sach Sahib Sacha Sachi Nai

Hai Bhi Hosi Jai Na Jasi Rachna Jis Rachai

Rangi Rangi Bhanti Kar Kar Jinsi Maya Jin Upayee

Kar Kar Vekhe Kita Aapna, Jiv Tis Di Vadiayee

Jo Tis Bhavai So Karsi Hukam Na Karna Jayee

So Patisah Saha Patisahib Nanak Rahan Rajai

Explanation

This Pauri gives wonderful description of the glory of Almighty. Similar description has been given in preceding Pauris in different ways and pattern.

It expresses where about and how is the Lord 's wonderful Mansion and His imperious thrown, from whence Almighty watch His creation and sustain it. That supreme location must be very mysterious from where Almighty monitor activities of His creation, preserve it and take care myracuously. Indirectly with great suspicion is being expressed that He must be within each one of His creation to look after to sustain and monitor. He cannot be external to His creation to take care so precisely. He has to be in each and every cell of His creation and with each breath of a created being. How wonderful is His mechanism and control, which is beyond the perception of a finite being. Each one of us exists within His regime, and His regime is within each one of us. In His wonderful regime there is variety of musical melodies and from where these innumerable melodies originate, is mysterious to conceive. Countless musical instruments are played by infinite number of musicians along with numerous fairies. All these musicians uninterruptly play divine melody and Ragas along with countless singers. It is being pointed here that in each breath of a creature Divine voice is going on, which is produced without striking of interacting surfaces. It is produced by calm flow breath by automatic breathing pattern and one needs to be in the state of absolute silence to be able to listen it. It is Divine Anahad Naad—the Divine voiceless voice. It is the melody of the Almighty. To be with this voiceless voice is like to be with Him. In other words, one can be with Almighty if he learns how to be in the divine temple of the Self. One need not to run in the out side world to find/discover Almighty. He rests in the Mansion of heart. To be with the Self is to be with the Almighty.

Furthermore, expressing the role of basic elements forming the human gross body, it is expressed that air, water, fire, are the fine constituents, jointly present along with the earth element in the body space. These elements have contradictory nature, fire burns, air spreads the fire but water extinguishes fire, but with all these contradictions in nature, the glory of virtues of Almighty through the melody of voiceless voice appears, and thus all these jointly adore the presence of Almighty in the gross body. It is the mystery of the mystery of the Supreme. If some one is chaste and pure in thoughts, he can easily feel as if Divine emperor of pure religious thoughts sings the Divine melodies in his heart that appears from the body gate—the mouth. He can never have thoughts of any type of vices. It is the wonderful experience of the presence of Divine power in one and all of us. It may also be said that air, water and fire appear to sing Divine melodies by their active flow and presence, as if "Dharam Raj'—the king of Divine purity is singing the Divine melodies at the door of Divinity where these demy gods of fire, water and air exist. It means all divine Devas/demy gods create divine melodies by themselves just merely by their presence. They are the religious leaders of the Universe, manage the universal activities by singing Divine songs, which appear from their mouths/gates automatically. It may also be said that gods of air, water, fire along with the god of death praise Almighty and in their praises, they try to merge in His glory

In each creation by the Almighty, in which the divine regime that exists, records all good and bad actions accomplished by the secret agency by name "Chitragupt". The role of this agency is not only to record the complete details of the action performed but also to examine whatsoever being written as per the divine Supernal laws, the net results of the fruits of the actions. This agency, the Chitragupt, has very responsible job, which is performed not mechanically but on getting merged/absorbed in the divine melodies while executing this job of deciding the fate of an individual. So that the every action and decision of an individual must always be under the supervision of the Almighty force. They uninterruptedly work and sing the glory of Almighty simultaneously, and not merely work or merely sing the Divine melodies. Furthermore, Lord Shiva, Lord Brahma, Parvati and Goddesses, all sing and adore the glory and virtues of Almighty. Their Divine existence is by the grace of Lord. Lord of heaven, the Indra, lording on his throne, sings Divine melodies along with various demy gods/Devas around and working under his supervision. Mergence in His glory is the sole aim of their praise for Him. The ascetics in their trance and holy devotees in deep Divine contemplation also sing His glory. Countless celibrate, and many virtuous, truthful, contented people and many valiant heroes always engage themselves in singing the divine glory in different melodies.

Vedic scholars and great-learned sages, Pundits exalt Almighty with their praises from generations. Bewitching maids of heaven, earth and nether regions too sing exalted Divine glory, which touches the sensitive hearts and one get easily absorb in the nectar of unimaginable Divinity and ecstasy. Also, gems created by the grace of Almighty along with the sixty-eight holy pilgrimages sing Him with great devotion. Valiant warriors of the universe sing His glory for the grace of Almighty for the power they are blessed with, as do all the four sources of this creation i.e. all those created either through Egg, through Womb, and through Sweat and Seed (although there are countless sources of creation but mainly these are the four categories that exist in this universe). All regions and Cosmic spheres of this universe adore His glory for their sustenance as a token of reverence towards Almighty. It is because of the fact that indeed it is a mystery of Almighty till date before scientists even to conceive the origin of great magnetic forces supporting and sustaining the huge planets and spheres in this Cosmos. Undoubtedly, all those adore Him who are graced by Him, and are immersed deeply in devotion to Him, sing His melodious glory. Without His Will and command, no one can sing His glory. Guru Nanak Ji says that how many more sing His glories are beyond reckoning, and are even beyond perception. Infinite has no boundary and it is beyond and beyond of expression and contemplation in the deep heart.

The lord of the Universe, the Almighty is eternal. His Name being is so ever true that He 'is' and will ever be. He is the One who is the cause of all creation. He is Changeless and beyond time. Being beyond time He is ever new and fresh, nothing can ever deteriorate Him. His truth-ness is His glory. His virtues and qualities are Eternal and beyond any change and expressions. He is beyond birth and death. Being Eternal, He is, He was and He will always remain with each one of us. He is eternal with His creation, and will remain forever with generations with His creation ever new. He Himself is the creator of Maya, the delusion, of diverse colors, hues and shades, which is constantly changing and never stable. Having created this Universe, which is ever changing and not stable, He watches His own handwork of creation as pleasing to His grandeur/magnificence. According to His magnificent dignity, He creates, watches and recreates. He is the observer and takes care of His creation as per His Wish. Almighty does what pleases to Him. No one can give any orders to Him. He himself is the Master. Guru Nanak Ji says that Lord, the Almighty is the king of kings. One must live as per His command and honor His Will.

In short, this Pauri expresses wonder, cosmic diversity of creation and affirms Almighty form to be infinite. He is formless but forms and shapes are His creation. His descriptions of glories are beyond expressions. Mergence in the glory of Almighty and get liberation is the sole aim of praises in different ways for Him by His creation.

Equivalent Verses of Srimad Bhagavad Gita (Pauri 27)

Chapter 9

The Royal Knowledge, The Royal Mystery

How the Lord Pervades All Creation, Yet Remains Transcendent (Verses 13-15)

महात्मानस्तु मां पार्थ दैवीं प्रकृतिमाश्रिताः ।
भजन्त्यनन्यमनसो ज्ञात्वा भूतादिमव्ययम् ।।१३।।

13. "But, O Parth, they who have found shelter in divine nature and know me as the eternal, imperishable source of all beings, worship me with perfect devotion."

सततं कीर्तयन्तो मां यतन्तश्च दृढव्रताः ।
नमस्यन्तश्च मां भक्त्या नित्ययुक्ता उपासते ।।१४।।

14. "Always engaged in the recital of my name and virtues, ever-active to realize me, and constantly offering obeisance to me, devotees with a firm determination worship me with undivided faith."

ज्ञानयज्ञेन चाप्यन्ये यजन्तो मामुपासते ।
एकत्वेन पृथक्त्वेन बहुधा विश्वतोमुखम् ।।१५।।

15. "While some worship me by gyan-yagya as the all-encompassing Supreme Spirit with the feeling that I am all, some worship me with a sense of identity, some with a sense of being separate from me (regarding me as master and themselves as servants), while yet others worship me in many a different fashion."

Pauri - 28

Explanation

In this Pauri the significance of meditation has been briefed as the path of Self-realization. As per system of Yoga various physical Asana are dealt in details for physical wellbeing and improvement of health. For mental wellbeing and spiritual up liftment, meditation, practice of Dhyana has been recommended in Indian System of Yogic Sciences.

As yama and Niyama are dealt in great details and great deal of importance is given in the improvement of life style before following the path of Ashtang yoga. Here in this Pauri the quality of mental contentment is given as the outstanding importance to follow the vertical journey to Almighty. It is expressed that contentment must become like the earrings, as the symbol of beauty, in the way of living. For external physical look/beauty, wearing of earrings is quite common, but it does not give any contentment and does not show the way to follow the Divine path. Instead of this, one must engage him in dignified labor to earn his living for self contentment. Or it may be said that one must live with modesty, with grace and self-respect. He must not do any such activity in his routine life such that his dignified grace gets affected. He must spend his part of life span apart from his daily earning in the meditation – to fix his life energies, his Dhyana, towards Almighty. He must put ashes of meditation/Dhyana on his mind and Chidakasa to get merge him in the glory of Almighty. As lord Shiva puts ashes of dead on his body so that he is always aware of/remembers death, which can come any time in life. One must have fear of death in his mind—in his thoughts. Fear of death must become the garments of his chaste body. It does not mean that one needs to be scared of death. On the contrary one must welcome death. To be always aware of death creates the feeling of dissipation, the Vairagaih in the heart. It must be silently active in the inner world of the devotee so that it becomes easy for him to be away from various vices of this world and he should be able to keep his body and mind completely chaste like a body of the virgin. This approach indeed helps to keep the control on sensual pleasure and one can easily observe Brahmcharya in his life. This is as per the system of yoga, which recommends practicing Pranayama to maintain purity in the system and in thoughts to lead pure, sin free and innocent life. His determination acts as the sectarian staff for his internal Divine progress. This facilitates to make fast progress towards spiritual Self-realization, to get merged in the glory of God. Spiritual experience of devotee by his efforts, thus achieved with time, must act as protection device like stick in the hands of security staff to keep him away from the attack of vices. Since attack of vices in one's life is a continuous process on the mind and it requires protection by spiritual experiences and by the grace of Almighty.

These first two lines of this Para can also be explained that by following the path of meditation for inner evolution and working with great honesty for earning lively hood, the strong life force and Divine energies appear in the human system, which cultivates in his mind all the 27 divine qualities as listed in Geeta including contentment, purity etc. With time Dissipation appear in the thoughts that make the devotee completely desire free, pure in all respects and one gets easily merged in the glory of the God. Thus one becomes Self-realized with time.

Further it is very vividly expressed that the path of divine following is the path of universal brotherhood. One must consider that all the creation of this universe are very closely knitted, they belong to the same class. There is no difference in their needs, however they may differ in their evolution. They all must be treated equally without any difference and disparities. The creation of whole universe belongs to one single cult only. There is no Diksha required. Taking birth in this Universe means that one is God's creation and belongs to the Divine cult only. If one really wants to conquer the world, the only way is to conquer his mind. To conquer the mind means to control his senses, to control his desires as if to control the flow of wind without walls. Thus, to control the mind and becomes thoughtless is more difficult than to conquer the world. However, it can be done by calming down the mind by purifying it, by dissolving the vices stored in it, removing the past Samaskaras in housed in the unconscious layers of mind by burning all of them in the fire created by chanting of Divine name, by meditation and absorption the Self in the glory of the Almighty. This all is feasible by His grace only. Allocation of life force and its revolving process in the human system leads to evolve the devotee and all this is achieved by self efforts of the devotee by his meditation and by His blessings.

Lastly, one must hail into the Universal Lord, who is Primal, Pure, without shape & form, and Eternal. Furthermore, He is forever and remains the same, perfect, completely integrated, unchanged, unaffected with time, and is beyond time and thus ever new and fresh.

In the nutshell, it can be said that Guru Nanak Ji redefines the personality of a Hindu yogi or a sanyasin as above. But still even today the Hindu yogis wears ear-rings (*munda*), adorns the loin cloth (*jholi*), carries a begging bowl (*khappar*) and a staff (*danda*). He also smears himself with ashes (*vibhuti*).

Rebuilding the image of a "Sikh" (one who is in search of Truth) - the Yogi, Guru Nanak asserts that contentment, modesty, contemplation, fear of death and a determined faith are necessary ingredients that guide a person to understand the path of Universal brotherhood and love. Conquering one's mind (the oscillation of thoughts) and by becoming determined to achieve God's realization and to put his whole energy for mergence in the divine glory only as a aim of life, one can conquer the world. In fact, the way of meditation is the only suggested means to be Self-realized in course of time by the grace of Cosmic power, the formless God.

Equivalent Verses of Srimad Bhagavad Gita (Pauri 28)

Chapter 12

Bhagti Yoga: Union Through Devotion

Qualities of the Devotee, Endearing to God (Verses 13-20)

अद्वेष्टा सर्वभूतानां मैत्रः करुण एव च ।
निर्ममो निरहङ्कारः समदुःखसुखः क्षमी ।।१३।।
सन्तुष्टः सततं योगी यतात्मा दृढनिश्चयः ।
मय्यर्पितमनोबुद्धिर्यो मद्भक्तः स मे प्रियः ।।१४।।

13-14. "The devotee who has malice towards none and loves all, who is compassionate and free from attachment and vanity, who views sorrow and joy equally and is forgiving, endowed with steady yog, contented alike with both profit and loss, restrained in mind, and dedicated to me with firm conviction, is dear to me."

यस्मान्नोद्विजते लोको लोकान्नोद्विजते च यः ।
हर्षामर्षभयोद्वेगैर्मुक्तो यः स च मे प्रियः ।।१५।।

15. "The devotee who does not upset anyone, nor is upset by anyone, and who is free from the contradictions of joy, envy, and fear, is dear to me."

अनपेक्षः शुचिर्दक्ष उदासीनो गतव्यथः ।
सर्वारम्भपरित्यागी यो मद्भक्तः स मे प्रियः ।।१६।।

16. "The devotee who is emancipated from desire, pure, dexterous at his task, impartial, free from sorrow, and who has achieved the state of actionlessness, is dear to me."

यो न हृष्यति न द्वेष्टि न शोचति न काङ्क्षति।
शुभाशुभपरित्यागी भक्तिमान्यः स मे प्रियः ।।१७।।

17. "The devotee who is neither joyous nor envious, neither troubled nor concerned, and who has given up all good and evil actions, is dear to me."

समः शत्रौ च मित्रे च तथा मानापमानयोः ।
शीतोष्णसुखदुःखेषु समः सङ्गविवर्जितः ।।१८।।
तुल्यनिन्दास्तुतिर्मौनी सन्तुष्टो येन केनचित् ।
अनिकेतः स्थिरमतिर्भक्तिमान्मे प्रियो नरः ।।१९।।

18-19. "The steady worshipper, who regards friends and foes, honour and dishonour, cold and heat, happiness and sorrow, as equal, and who is detached from the world, indifferent to slander and praise, meditative, contented with any manner of physical sustenance, and free from infatuation for the place where he dwells, is dear to me.

ये तु धर्म्यामृतमिदं यथोक्तं पर्युपासते।
श्रद्दधाना मत्परमा भक्तास्तेऽतीव मे प्रियाः ।।२०।।

20. "And the devotees who rest in me and taste well the aforesaid nectar of dharm in a spirit of selflessness are the dearest to me."

Chapter 14

Transcending The Gunas

Mixture of Good and Evil in Human Nature (Verses 10-13)

रजस्तमश्चाभिभूय सत्त्वं भवति भारत ।
रज: सत्त्वं तमश्चैव तम: सत्त्वं रजस्तथा ।।१०।।

10. "And, O Bharat, (just as) sattwa grows by overcoming the properties of rajas and tamas, tamas grows by overpowering rajas and sattwa, and the property of rajas grows by suppressing tamas and sattwa."

सर्वद्वारेषु देहेऽस्मिन्प्रकाश उपजायते ।
ज्ञानं यदा तदा विद्याद्विवृद्धं सत्त्वमित्युत ।।११।।

11. "When the mind and senses are suffused with the light of knowledge and consciousness, it should be taken as a sign of the growing strength of sattwa."

लोभ: प्रवृत्तिरारम्भ: कर्मणाशाम: स्पृहा ।
रजस्येतानि जायन्ते विवृद्धे भरतर्षभ ।।१२।।

12. "When the property of rajas is ascendant, O the best of Bharat, greed, worldly inclination, the tendency to undertake action , restlessness, and desire for sensual pleasures arise."

अप्रकाशोऽप्रवृत्तिश्च प्रमादो मोह एव च ।
तमस्येतानि जायन्ते विवृद्धे कुरुनन्दन ।।१३।।

13. "When there is an upsurge of tamas, O Kurunandan, darkness, disinclination to duty which ought to be done, carelessness, and tendencies that engender infatuation arise."

Pauri - 29

Explanation

Gross food is required to sustain the physical body, to make it healthy and keep it going. Gross food cannot give the required nourishment to the mind that gives mental health, happiness, contentment and other required prerequisite for its well -being. The food of the mind is divine knowledge. The divine knowledge gives the virtue & quality of compassion to the mind, which is the resultant of the accumulated, perceived and practice of divine activities in the real life. Compassion is the essence /grace of the Almighty as the resultant of the fruit of mergence in His divine glory. Compassion is the treasure of the divine food; it is like steward of divine knowledge. During the process of consumption and accumulation of divine knowledge in the mental frame, divine melody in the physical human temple is uninterruptedly goes on with each inflow and outflow of the breath. It is such a fine voiceless voice that ear is unable to make a note of this, but with complete silence of mind and on being attentive within, this celestial melody can be easily conceived, felt, tasted and enjoyed that vibrates in the heart and in the fine human body. This makes the devotee to express the omnipresence of Almighty and His omnipotent nature.

Almighty is the Lord who rules the whole Universe. He is the Master of the whole creation. He takes the net command and responsibility to govern each one of us in all conditions. Almighty controls us similar to the bull master, who after putting rope in the nose of the bull controls completely all his actions. Under these conditions bull cannot move in a haphazard way of his own. His master, who has rope in his hand to have absolute control, governs his every step. In the same way one can control his mind provided he succeeds to manage to keep his senses under his thumb.

Furthermore, various problems faced by spiritual aspirant have been brought in this Pauri. It is said that different types of powers to perform miracles and different types of occult capabilities, which one gets during the process of spiritual efforts, are hindrance in the ultimate goal of Self –realization, and are simply useless and act as obstacles in the divine path. The taste /use of these powers ruin the progress of the spiritual aspirants. One must not show spiritual miracles to others to demonstrate for any purpose, relevant or irrelevant. These powers if used for undue gains, ruin the developed spiritual capabilities of devotees and don't allow him to make progress in the path of divinity, rather the accumulated grace of Almighty is washed away automatically with time. These powers are for different class of people who have low mentality. Spiritual aspirants must look for the mergence in

Almighty, to taste His magnificence, and aim only for realization of the Self within.

As in our body system, breath in and breath out goes on continuously, similarly a type of Pranayama goes on in this magnificent universe. The process of breath in and out are similar to birth and death, and this process is continued for each one of us in this universal creation. As night goes, day comes. Similarly day goes and night comes. This is uninterrupted process and is as per the divine law and system of Almighty. No one can interfere in this. Thus, these two one after the other is like union and separation, are like two wheels of the universe that churn the share of destiny of the creation. One gets and loses as per his prewritten destiny. There may be union or separation, whatsoever is destined, is ought to happen. Only Almighty can alter if He Wishes. Life and death, happiness and miseries, loss and gain, likes and dislike, union and separation, hot and cold weather, friendship and enmity and all other processes are duality of life. Life moves in duality. It is the unaltered law of nature. Along with many other conditions, the law of action and reaction play a major significant role. This all is basically governed by omnipresent and omniscient power of Almighty.

Lastly, one must hail into the Universal Lord, who is Primal, Pure, without shape & form, and Eternal. Furthermore, He is forever and remains the same, perfect, completely integrated, unchanged, unaffected with time, and is beyond time and thus ever new and fresh.

In this Pauri in the nutshell, expanding upon the previous one, Guru Nanak Ji shuns the Yogi who is engaged in acquiring occult powers to perform miracles. He preaches that the sole purpose of a Yogi should be a communion with the Divine spirit and not to get trapped in occult powers. Duality is a universal law. If one expects and wishes happiness in life then he must be prepared for sorrow. This continued universal divine process must be honored.

Equivalent Verses of Srimad Bhagavad Gita (Pauri 29)

Chapter 5

Freedom Through Inner Renunciation

Which is Better: Serving in the World or Seeking Wisdom in Seculation? (Verses 1-3)

सन्न्यासं कर्मणां कृष्ण पुनर्योगं च शंससि।
यच्छ्रेय एतयोरेकं तन्मे ब्रूहि सुनिश्चितम्।।१।।

1. "Arjun said, 'You have so far commended, O Krishn, both the Way of knowledge through Renunciation and then the Way of Selfless Action; so now tell me which one of the two is decidedly more propitious.'"

सन्न्यासः कर्मयोगश्च निः श्रेयसकरावुभौ।
तयोस्तु कर्मसन्न्यासात्कर्मयोगो विशिष्यते।।२।।

2. "The Lord said, 'Both renunciation and selfless action achieve salvation, but of the two the Way of Selfless Action is the better because it is easier to practise.'"

ज्ञेयः स नित्यसन्न्यासी यो न द्वेष्टि न काङ्क्षति।
निर्द्वन्द्वो हि महाबाहो सुखं बन्धात्प्रमुच्यते।।३।।

3. "He, O the mighty-armed (Arjun), who envies none and desires nothing is fit to be regarded as a true sanyasi and, liberated from the conflicts of passion and repugnance, he breaks away from worldly bondage."

Chapter 2

Sankhya And Yoga: Cosmic Wisdom And The Method Of Attainment

The Eternel, Transcendental Nature of the Soul (Verses 26-27)

अथ चैनं नित्यजातं नित्यं वा मन्यसे मृतम्।
तथापि त्वं महाबाहो नैवं शोचितुमर्हसि।।२६।।

26. "You ought not to grieve, O the mighty-armed, even if you think of him (the Self) as ever-born and ever-dying."

जातस्य हि ध्रुवो मृत्युर्ध्रुवं जन्म मृतस्य च।
तस्मादपरिहार्येऽर्थे न त्वं शोचितुमर्हसि।।२७।।

27. "Since this also proves the certain death of what is born and the certain birth of what dies, you ought not to grieve over the inevitable."

Pauri - 30

Explanation

The Supreme spirit, the Almighty, has created/manifested the Maya, the delusion, which is ever changing and always-in transient mode. Maya is contradictory in virtues and qualities to Supernal, which is changeless and ever fresh and new. Maya is like a mother that gets conceived, and delivers by mysterious divine provisions. In this universe, the Maya—the mother conceived and delivered Holy Triad, which is the clear direct evidence of the Creator. Since the Triad is through the mother Maya and so is in the transient state, in the state of change. The Triad, which is through the mother Maya, is the Creator, the Sustainer and the Destroyer. As per Hindu mythology, they are Brahma, Vishnu and Mahesh. The Brahma is the creator of the world, Vishnu is preserver, the retainer and Shiva is the judge to decide to take final decision to destroy/merge the creation so as to complete the circuit of birth, life and death. Thus, this is the continued repeated time cycle like a moving wheel. Almighty is the observer in this play of the Triad. This is an extremely mysterious provision of Almighty where He is just being the observer without any of His participation. It is mysterious delivery by the Maya, the mother, and the mysterious wonderful process by which the Maya is conceived. This is the mystery of mystery of Maya and Her power that created from herself the three virtues namely Satva—the Brahma, Rajasva—the Vishnu, and Tamasa—the Shiva. Almighty is supreme and above all these virtues. Almighty closely observe these virtues but do not participate to cultivate them. This mystery is beyond of beyond to perceive. All these three forces are created by Maya but are under Almighty, He is silent, knowable but yet unknown.

With all this as expressed above, Almighty ordains as pleases Him for the Triad to act. He assigns the activities either to Brahma, to Vishnu or to Shiva as He likes or conceives on probing into infinity. His command in all universal affairs are only His and beyond and beyond even to apprehend. No body can see but He sees all. His actions and His divine command and plans, only He knows. This is and this will remain the greatest wonder of the universe. He is completely aware of present, past and future, but none is aware of Almighty—the Supreme power.

Lastly, one must hail into the Universal Lord, who is Primal, Pure, without shape & form, and Eternal. Furthermore, He is forever and remains the same, perfect, completely integrated, unchanged, unaffected with time, and is beyond time and thus ever new and fresh.

Equivalent Verses of Srimad Bhagavad Gita (Pauri 30)

Chapter 7

The Nature Of Spirit And Spirit Of Nature

Cosmic Hypnosis (Maya) and the Way to Transcend It (Verses 13-15)

त्रिभिर्गुणमयैर्भावैरेभिः सर्वमिदं जगत्।
मोहितं नाभिजानाति मामेभ्यः परमव्ययम्।।१३।।

13. "Since the whole world is deluded by feelings resulting from the operation of the three properties, it is unaware of my imperishable essence that is beyond them."

दैवी ह्येषा गुणमयी मम माया दुरत्यया।
मामेव ये प्रपद्यन्ते मायामेतां तरन्ति ते।।१४।।

14. "This divine three-propertied yog-maya of mine is most difficult to overcome, but they who seek refuge in me get over the illusion and achieve salvation.

न मां दुष्कृतिनो मूढाः प्रपद्यन्ते नराधमाः।
माययापहृतज्ञाना आसुरं भावमाश्रिताः।।१५।।

15. "The ignorant and unwise are the most despicable of men and doers of wickedness, because deluded by maya and having demoniacal qualities they do not worship me."

Pauri - 31

Explanation

This Pauri expresses the omnipresence status of Almighty, and, as well, His treasures, which is present everywhere throughout the universe. By His treasures of divine qualities, virtues as well as in the form of material goods, He has spread Himself all around in the universe even in the fine bodies of His creations and in the smallest tiny spaces. His stocked, His grace in both seen and unseen forms in every store /house pervading in entire universe. Every storehouse is being operated by His unending Blessings. Whatsoever He gifts by His grace that endures forever for one's needs. In other words, once He gives it will be continued. Once He graces His devotee by His enlightenment/realization, this will be everlasting. The divine light will remains and it will never extinguish. His stock of divine grace and material goods endure beyond time, and there will never be any shortage of any type. Almighty creates by Himself and beholds the view. He is the originator, creator, the preserver, and sustainer of the universe. For Him the creation, observation and maintenance of the universe is the continuous process till His creation is completed. He acts like an artist, who creates, closely observes His art, modifies it as per His wish till He is satisfied with His art and considers it to be completed. It may be perceived that Almighty graces with His enlightenment to His beloved devotee and observes His progress in this miraculous divine path till the Lord is fully satisfied with the progress of the devotee. Until then Almighty closely observes him and keeps him in close supervision to make him as perfect as is He.

Guru Nanak Ji says that Almighty is Truth, changeless and beyond time. His whole creation is truth. His creation cannot be untruth and false. Truth always represent truth, since Almighty is truth so every thing concerning Him, linked with Him has to be true only. From truth exists the creation, which is true.

Lastly, it is said that one must hail into the Universal Lord, who is Primal, Pure, without shape & form, and Eternal. Furthermore, He is forever and remains the same, perfect, completely integrated, unchanged, unaffected with time, and is beyond time and thus ever new and fresh.

In the nutshell this Pauri asserts that God pervades in the entire universe that is His own creation. And this universe is real and not an illusion to be shunned. It clearly explains that He created the Universe (the storehouse) in such a manner that in its own cyclic way, it is filled always with infinite bounties, and also, the entire Universe is the infinite form of God.

Equivalent Verses of Srimad Bhagavad Gita (Pauri 31)

Chapter 7

The Nature Of Spirit And Spirit Of Nature

How the Creator Sustains the Manifested Creation (Verses 10-12)

बीजं मां सर्वभूतानां विद्धि पार्थ सनातनम् ।
बुद्धिर्बुद्धिमतामस्मि तेजस्तेजस्विनामहम् ।।१०।।

10. "Since l am also the intellect in wise men and the magnificence of men of glory, know you, O Arjun, that I am the eternal fountainhead of all beings.

बलं बलवतां चाहं कामरागविवर्जितम् ।
धर्माविरुद्धो भूतेषु कामोऽस्मि भरतर्षभ ।।११।।

11. "I am, O the best of Bharat, the selfless power of the strong and I, too, am the aspiration for realization in all beings that is never hostile to God."

ये चैव साच्त्विका भावा राजसास्तामसाश्च ये ।
मत्त एवेति तान्विद्धि न त्वहं तेषु ते मयि ।।१२।।

12. "And know that although all the properties of nature (tamas, rajas and sattwa) have arisen from me, they neither dwell in me nor do I dwell in them."

Pauri - 32

Explanation

In this Pauri, Guru Nanak lays emphasis on *Simran* or continuous repetition of the divine Name/japa of God, so that one gets merge in His glory. Only then it is possible to achieve the union with the beloved Almighty as if He and the devotee are the same.

Devotee prays that instead of one tongue, if the tongue may become multifold to become a Lakh in number, and then one Lakh may turn to twenty times (twenty Lakhs) in number, he will continue to repeat the name/japa of Almighty, in this way by countless tongues in countless times i.e. lakhs and lakhs times (million of times). The continuous reciting His name and then completing getting merge in the name of His glory, one enters in the state of Samadhi, which gives intrinsic enlightenment, is the spiritual effort, the Sadhana, of a devotee. This Simran alone is the ladder to ascend, and to merge and enjoy the joy of mergence with Almighty. In other words instead of having million tongues, even twenty time of this score, and with these tongues reciting His glorious name over and over, creates divine energy, which merges the individual consciousness of a devotee with the Supernal consciousness, and thus he enjoys the joy of self-realization.

In the same way, Guru Nanak Ji hints that the joint recitation of divine glory, by countless tongues has much more significant effect than that by an individual of his single tongue. Joint recitation charges the environment and consequently the human system with high frequency divine energy in a shorter span, which makes easier to climb the ladder of divinity. Having multifold tongues has the intrinsic meaning to have joint recitation with devotion, which has multifold effect in the shorter span. However, just recitation of God's name mechanically without the involvement of one's mind, is just a physical exercise and does not fetch any benefit to climb the ladder of self-realization. Such are just the futile efforts to boost the self- egoism before others. These approaches are just for the false projection of self- greatness before the fellow-beings without enhancing the self-purity and developing the love for Almighty.

The mergence in the divine glory dissolves the self- egoism, and creates the purity in thoughts, words and deeds. Simply recitation without mind, devotion and self-involvement are just the physical mechanical false approach and futile efforts, and if one considers these efforts to get the Blessings of Almighty, then it is his false egoism, and nothing beyond this.

One must remember that grace of the Almighty is by His grace only, and not merely by self-efforts. After immense self-efforts in this direction, one finally understands that efforts are just the means but mergence in infinite is by the mercy of infinite.

The path of vertical journey by a devotee sky-ward towards the mergence in the beauty of Almighty, and listening to His wonderful mysterious divine stories and getting divine experiences attract many people around, who have just taken human birth from the animal origin, being not yet sufficiently spiritually evolved, they try to copy such devotees to follow the divine path to get accelerated evolution to be self-realized. This also means that by hearing the heavenly words, even the meanest worm is tempted to soar to climb this divine ladder. Guru Nanak Ji says that by His grace alone the God is attained, and all other means lacking His grace are false and are in vain, which do not get any divine benefit to such devotees.

Equivalent Verses of Srimad Bhagavad Gita (Pauri 32)

Chapter 12

Bhagti Yoga, Union Through Devotion

Should the Yogi Worship the Unmanifest, or a Personal God? (Verses 1-4)

अर्जुन उवाच
एवं सततयुक्ता ये भक्तास्त्वां पर्युपासते।
ये चाप्यक्षरमव्यक्तं तेषां के योगवित्तमाः ॥१॥

1. "Arjun said, 'Which of the two kinds of steadfast devotees, they who always worship you in your embodied form and the others who meditate upon your imperishable, unmanifest Spirit, are superior in their mastery of yog?' "

मय्यावेश्य मनो ये मां नित्ययुक्ता उपासते।
श्रद्धया परयोपेतास्ते मे युक्ततमा मताः ॥२॥

2. "The Lord said, 'I believe them to be the most superior of all yogi who always meditate upon me with concentration and worship me (the embodied, manifest God) with true faith.' "

ये त्वक्षरमनिर्देश्यमव्यक्तं पर्युपासते।
सर्वत्रगमचिन्त्यं च कूटस्थमचलं ध्रुवम् ॥३॥
सन्नियम्येन्द्रियग्रामं सर्वत्र समबुद्धयः।
ते प्राप्नुवन्ति मामेव सर्वभूतहिते रताः ॥४॥

3-4. "And they who restrain all their senses well, always adore the Supreme Spirit who is beyond thought, all-pervading, indefinable, filled with equanimity, immutable and immovable, and formless and indestructible , with total concentration, and who serve all beings viewing them with an equal eye, attain to me."

Pauri - 33

Explanation

In this Pauri, Guru Nanak Ji categorically explains that nothing is in one's own power. And no one in himself is superior or inferior. Everything is in the control of Almighty including that of his intention and thinking. Sooner one learns/ understands in totality that except surrendering to Him there is no alternative, better it will be for him, in all respects and in all walks of life to surrender to Almighty.

We are literally so powerless that by our own ego, we can neither speak or nor can remain/observe silence. To speak and to remain silent, both the faculties are in the control of Almighty, the Supernal. Since human mind being abstract source of power, is linked with soul, which is integrated with the Supernal. So, as He Wishes, a creature has to act accordingly. His ways of control are mysterious and beyond the perception of human being. We being powerless on both the fronts to receive or to bestow, have only futile ego.

One does not basically has any say/power to beg from Almighty and nor has any say to offer any thing to Him. One does not take birth as per his wish and nor leave the world as he desires. Birth and death are as per His command and are beyond one's power. Based on one's activity and hard work, one cannot earn wealth and neither can enjoy the kingly power, although one's heart and mind long for these gains throughout his life, and he leaves no stone unturned to get glory of power and wealth. In fact neither riches and nor mental turbulence are in one's power. One can accumulate wealth /riches and peace of mind only by His grace. One can only do his duty but any blessing or grace either worldly or divine; both are as per Almighty's Wish. One must work for the work sake and leave results/fruits of his work in the hands of Almighty. This is the only key of success, happiness and joy in life. One's fate and past karmas/actions play a major role to decide the fate and to get the grace of divine blessings. One revolves around the final command of Almighty Will and his own reactions of the past actions.

Furthermore, awareness and awakening are not in one's capability, and neither to follow the path of liberation is in one's power. By one's own power, it is not possible to gain knowledge of any kind, adore Almighty and merge in deep contemplation of His divine glory. Even to put sincere efforts for liberations are also not in the purview of one's approach. Unless and until God inspire for any of the divine activities, one cannot think even to commence. Almighty is the spirit and basic force for all human thinking and activities. Only God has the power to behold. No one is great/nice/good and also no one is small/bad by himself or herself. Almighty

Himself is the force and power that make one uplifted by performing his activities or fill his mind with divine contemplation. This is the great play of Almighty. It is similar to the waves in the ocean, one wave might go high and other may die down without gaining any height. Thus all the glories one bestows in his life, is just by the grace of Almighty. God is omnipresent observer and this world is the child's play/ drama for Him, where one needs to act as per the role given by the Supernal / Master of the universe. As per Guru Nanak Ji, none is high or none is low, all is by Almighty's will and the role assigned by Him in this play/drama. However, one's serious and sincere efforts play a significant role to uplift an individual by God's grace.

In the nutshell, in our day-to-day life, we are governed by our ego and ever-changing mental conditions. This is so as we are bound by Time, Space and Causation. Yet, we in our ignorance feel that we have "power" to do this or do that and become boastful of our "power". This ignorance leads us to feel ourselves superior to others. But in reality, all is governed by His power and force. As we realize this in our life, we surrender to Him in totality. Our egoism vanishes. When we perceive that He is the force behind every movement, and by merely our efforts we cannot achieve Him, then only divine enlightenment pours in our consciousness and gradually we become self-realized. If one can achieve Almighty by His efforts, it would mean that individual efforts are bigger than His force. By efforts, when we become effortless and efforts no way help us, then and then only as per His Wish, He may bless us with His grace. We are always at His mercy. Basically, we are powerless and only can pray for His mercy and Blessings. In other prospective, this Pauri brings that one must be desire less and all the activities to be devoted to Him only. No desire means no requirements and no command, and no mental force to achieve, and finally total surrender to Him for the Self-realization and ultimate happiness.

Equivalent Verses of Srimad Bhagavad Gita (Pauri 33)

Chapter 12

Bhagti Yoga, Union Through Devotion

The Levels of Spiritual practice and the Stages of Realization (Verses 8-12)

मय्येव मन आधत्स्व मयि बुद्धिं निवेशय।
निवसिष्यसि मय्येव अत ऊर्ध्वं न संशयः ॥८॥

8. "There is no doubt whatsoever that you will dwell in me if you devote and apply your mind and intellect to me."

अथ चित्तं समाधातुं न शक्नोषि मयि स्थिरम्।
अभ्यासयोगेन ततो मामिच्छाप्तुं धनञ्जय ॥९॥

9. "If you cannot firmly set your mind on me; O Dhananjay, seek me by the yog of incessant practice (abhyas-yog)."

अभ्यासेऽप्यसमर्थोऽसि मत्कर्मपरमो भव।
मदर्थमपि कर्माणि कुर्वन्सिद्धिमवाप्स्यसि ॥१०॥

10. "In case you are incapable of even following the way of practice, you may yet secure fulfillment by the performance of actions which are meant only for me."

अथैतदप्यशक्तोऽसि कर्तुं मद्योगमाश्रितः।
सर्वकर्मफलत्यागं ततः कुरु यतात्मवान् ॥११॥

11. "In case you fail to accomplish even this, abandon all the fruits of action and rake refuge in my yog with a thoroughly subdued mind."

श्रेयो हि ज्ञानमभ्यासाज्ज्ञानाद्ध्यानं विशिष्यते।
ध्यानात्कर्मफलत्यागस्त्यागाच्छान्तिरनन्तरम् ।।१२।।

12. "Since knowledge is superior to practice, meditation better than knowledge, and abandonment of the fruits of action higher than meditation, renunciation is soon rewarded with peace."

Chapter 14

Transcending The Gunas

The Nature of the Jivanmukta – One Who Rises Above Nature's Qualities (Verses 19-27)

नान्यं गुणेभ्यः कर्तारं यदा द्रष्टानुपश्यति।
गुणेभ्यश्च परं वेत्ति मद्भावं सोऽधिगच्छति ।।१९।।

19. "When the Soul (that is a mere witness) does not see anyone besides the three properties as doer and when he knows the essence of the Supreme Spirit who is beyond these properties, he attains to my state."

गुणानेतानतीत्य त्रीन्देही देहसमुद्भवान्।
जन्ममृत्युजरादुःखैर्विमुक्तोऽमृतमश्नुते ।।२०।।

20. 'Transcending the properties that are the germ of the gross, corporal body and liberated from the miseries of birth, death, and old age, the Soul achieves the ultimate bliss."

कैर्लिङ्गैस्त्रीन्गुणानेतानतीतो भवति प्रभो।
किमाचारः कथं चैतांस्त्रीन्गुणानतिवर्तते।।२१।।

21. "Arjun said, '(Tell me), O Lord, the attributes of the man who has risen above the three properties, his manner of life, and the way by which he transcends the three properties.'"

प्रकाशं च प्रवृत्ति च मोहमेव च पाण्डव।
न द्वेष्टि सम्प्रवृत्तानि न निवृत्तानि काङ्क्षति।।२२।।

22. "The Lord said, 'The man, O Pandav, who neither abhors radiance, inclination to action, and attachment that are generated respectively by the operations of sattwa, rajas, and tamas when he is involved in them, nor aspires for them when he is liberated;...'"

उदासीनवदासीनो गुणैर्यो न विचाल्यते।
गुणा वर्तन्त इत्येव योऽवतिष्ठति नेङ्गते।।२३।।

23. "(And) who, like a dispassionate onlooker, is unmoved by the properties and is steady and unshaken by dint of his realization that these properties of nature but abide in themselves;..."

समदुःखसुखः स्वस्थः समलोष्टाश्मकाञ्चनः।
तुल्यप्रियाप्रियो धीरस्तुल्यनिन्दात्मसंस्तुतिः।।२४।।

24. "(And) who, ever dwelling in his Self, views joy, sorrow, earth, stone, and gold as equal, is patient, and evenly regards the pleasant and the unpleasant, slander and praise;..."

मानापमानयोस्तुल्यस्तुल्यो मित्रारिपक्षयोः।
सर्वारम्भपरित्यागी गुणातीतः स उच्यते।।२५।।

25. "(And) who puts up with honour and dishonour, as (also) with friend and foe, with equanimity, and who gives up the undertaking of action is said to have transcended all the properties."

मां च योऽव्यभिचारेण भक्तियोगेन सेवते।
स गुणान्समतीत्यैतान्ब्रह्मभूयाय कल्पते।।२६।।

26. "And the man who serves me with the yog of unswerving devotion overcomes the three properties and secures the state of oneness with God."

ब्रह्मणो हि प्रतिष्ठाहममृतस्याव्ययस्य च।
शाश्वतस्य च धर्मस्य सुखस्यैकान्तिकस्य च।।२७।।

27. "For I am the one in which the eternal God, immortal life, the imperishable dharm, and the ultimate bliss all (abide)."

Pauri - 34

Explanation

Almighty by His magnificent power has created nights, days, seasons, dates and weeks (different days of a week) to revolve the time around its own axis. With certain set pattern these are repeating by their own way as per the command of the nature. Also God has created air, water, fire and nether regions to assist the natural cycle to exist, operate and revolve for the survival of species of creation and well being besides various different mysterious purposes of their existence. In the timeless natural cycle and in between the two nether regions one below us and another above us i.e. sky, the Lord installed amidst both of them the mother earth, the place for the transient travelers/species to this universe for a short stay, on which this creation of the Almighty exists/survives.

This earth is also a place to execute karma/actions and Dharma/religious activities; wherein abide the multitude of species of infinite hues and forms. Almighty has created this small region of earth amidst infinite cosmic space and in timeless infinite (beyond time) so that His creation of multitude of species adores Him on taking birth in this region. God has created infinite species with infinite kinds, types, nature and mental inclination/built up. Creation of Almighty is of countless varieties, name and form. By His grace and Will a creature takes birth on this earth for performing virtuous actions to get merge in the glory of Almighty.

The various actions performed by these species during the time span of their existence/life on this earth are closely monitored/examined by the mysterious means of Almighty. The judgment by the Lord is always on the basis of truth and on the truthful facts since God is truth, unchanged, beyond time, ever fresh and new, so is His true court, and His judges as well His judgments. In His true court only saints are honored and are given the respectful position to judge as per the divine laws. They have divine approved respectful look that bears the mark of grace of the master. True from the false is completely screened there and these divine saints only honor truth.

Guru Nanak Ji says that the Almighty knows the intentions and complete mental in-built inclination of an individual and do not accept/value the false outward presentation. Almighty is clearly aware of the perfection and imperfection of an individual and decides his fate/destiny accordingly without any false/wrong projection but based on His true judgment/

evaluation. World is not aware of the intention of an individual behind his action, these might be selfish and harmful to others. Also, these might be misleading. Only divine cóurt can give the appropriate decision of such actions. Man made judgments can never be correct in the court of divinity. That is why Christ has said, which is the famous proverb in Christianity i.e. "Judge not, that Thee be not Judged". It means don't judge others, you will not be correct, and you will be judged.

The essence of this Pauri establishes the concept of the land of human action, the "*Karmbhoomi*". Man's very sojourn/stay or life span on earth is for actions and their experience. One has to justify his very existence on earth through faithful performance of duties assigned to him by Almighty, and March towards his onward vertical spiritual journey for God realization. The divine laws judge all actions of an individual so that he must cultivate virtues and a persistent endeavor to win the Divine Grace to be self-realized.

Equivalent Verses of Srimad Bhagavad Gita (Pauri 34)

Chapter 3

Karma Yoga: The Path Of Spiritual Action

Righteous Duty, Performed With Nonattachment, Is Godly (Verses 19-20)

तस्मादसक्त: सततं कार्यं कर्म समाचर ।
असक्तो ह्याचरन्कर्म परमाप्नोति पूरुष: ।।१९।।

19. "So always do what is right for you to do in the spirit of selflessness, for in doing his duty the selfless man attains to God."

कर्मणैव हि संसिद्धिमास्थिता जनकादय: ।
लोकसङ्ग्रहमेवापि सम्पश्यन्कर्तुमर्हसि ।।२०।।

20. "Since sages such as Janak had also attained to the ultimate realization by action, and keeping in mind, the preservation of the (God made) order, it is incumbent upon you to act."

Pauri 35

Explanation

In the earlier sections as above, the realm of religion/ Dharma is dealt in great details. The importance of religious, pure and moral living, following the path of "Yama" and "Niyama" that one must be adhered through out the life for spiritual enlistment, is manifested as the basic prerequisite of a devotee for the divine life. In the modern life this may be termed as moral way of living. To live as per moral codes, to follow moral ethics, to conduct oneself truthfully, to follow moral discrimination and as well differentiate between truth and false, are the religious way of living. This leads to sharpen the intellect of devotee, to make him pure in thoughts, which increases the intellectual power to grasp the divine knowledge. From this junction onwards, wisdom and intellectual capabilities to feel and digest the divine knowledge of a devotee commences, and he advances on the divine path without much effort by the automatic grasping of the mysterious divine abstract wisdom. He enters from the religious way of living to the divine knowledge base way of living and now his life dwells on the realm of pure knowledge. He clearly conceives that the purpose of life is not material collection and their utilization, but the main aim is cultivation of divinity, and to move to the goal of self-realization.

This makes him self-less and all his activities revolve around for the welfare of the fellow beings. This increases joy in his life. He gets contentment in giving and not in accumulating for the self. The divine knowledge gradually turns him to be saint like in thoughts, words and deeds. With time he becomes completely refined and perfect. All vices in mind of a devotee totally vanish with time. His mind gets merge in formless God, and he becomes Jeewan Mukta, the liberated soul in this life itself.

In continuation to this, the form of this infinite universe is expressed in a wonderful way. There are countless forms of fire, air and water in this vast universe. Also, there are infinite Krishanas and Shivas including countless Brahmas those creating myriad forms, shapes and colorful species in this universe. In this infinite creation of Almighty, there are countless earths, fields and mountains for activities besides countless sages like Dhruva with sermons and their wonderful sayings for the enlightenment of human beings. There is no count in this universe for Indras, Moons, and Suns and there are countless stellar and earthy regions. Furthermore, countless are Sidhas, Buddhas, Nathas and different form of Goddesses. There are infinite deities, demons & saints and countless jewels in the oceans. It is impossible to count the sources of creation, innumerable languages and many varieties of dynasties of kings in the universe. Guru Nank Ji says, there is no end to count the number of scriptures and their adherents. In deed, there is just no end of scope and vastness of this universal creation of Almighty.

The inner meaning of the Saying of Guru Nanak Ji in this Pauri is taken as the manifestation of the intellect of devotee by the divine knowledge/wisdom when he starts visualizing that this vast universe is like huge family where each one is made for each other. Everyone acts and fulfills the needs of others and in turn his needs are fulfilled. This is the mysterious mystery of Almighty and finite human mind wonders and wonders to visualize this mystery by the divine wisdom and adore Almighty and try to get merge in His glory.

Equivalent Verses of Srimad Bhagavad Gita (Pauri 35)

Chapter 10

The Infinite Manifestation Of The Unmanifest Spirit

I Will Tell Thee of My Phenomenal Expressions (Verses 19-42)

हन्त ते कथयिष्यामि दिव्या ह्यात्मविभूतयः।
प्राधान्यतः कुरुश्रेष्ठ नास्त्यन्तो विस्तरस्य मे।।१९।।

19. "The Lord (then) said, I shall now tell you of the power of my glories, for there is no end to my diverse manifestations."

अहमात्मा गुडाकेश सर्वभूताशयस्थितः।
अहमादिश्च मध्यं च भूतानामन्त एव च।।२०।।

20. "1 am, O Gudakesh, the Self that dwells within all beings, as also their primeval beginning, middle, and end."

आदित्यानामहं विष्णुर्ज्योतिषां रविरंशुमान्।
मरीचिर्मरुतामस्मि नक्षत्राणामहं शशी।।२१।।

21. "I am Vishnu among the twelve sons of Aditi, the sun among lights, the god Mareechi among winds, and the sovereign moon among planets."

वेदानां सामवेदोऽस्मि देवानामस्मि वासवः।
इन्द्रियाणां मनश्चास्मि भूतानामस्मि चेतना।।२२।।

22. "I am also the Sam among the Ved, Indr among gods, the mind among senses, and the consciousness in beings."

स्थाणां शंकरश्चास्मि वित्तेशो यक्षरक्षसाम् ।
वसूनां पावकश्चास्मि मेरू शिखरिणामहम् ॥२३॥

23. "I am Shankar among Rudr, Kuber among demons and yaksh, fire among Vasu, and the Sumeru among lofty mountains."

पुरोधसां च मुख्यं मां विद्धि पार्थ बृहस्पतिम् ।
सेनानीनामहं स्कन्दः सरसामस्मि सागरः ॥२४॥

24. "Be it known to you, Parth, that I am among priests the Chief Priest Brihaspati, Skand among martial chiefs, and the ocean among seas."

महर्षीणां भृगुरहं गिरामस्म्येकमक्षरम् ।
यज्ञानां जपयज्ञोऽस्मि स्थावराणां हिमालयः ॥२५॥

25. "I am Bhrigu among the great saints (maharshi), OM among words, the yagya of intoned prayers (jap-yagya) among yagya, and the Himalaya among stationary objects.

अश्वत्थः सर्ववृक्षाणां देवर्षीणां च नारदः ।
गन्धर्वाणां चित्ररथः सिद्धानां कपिलो मुनिः ॥२६॥

26. I am Ashwath (the Peepal) among trees, Narad among divine sages, Chitrarath among Gandharv, and the sage Kapil among men of attainment."

उच्चैःश्रवसमश्वानां विद्धि माममृतोद्भवम् ।
ऐरावतं गजेन्द्राणां नराणां च नराधिपम् ॥२७॥

27. "Know (also) that I am the nectar-born Uchchaishrav among horses, Airawat among pachyderms, and king among men."

आयुधानामहं वज्रं धेनूनामस्मि कामधुक्।
प्रजनश्चास्मि कन्दर्पः सर्पाणामस्मि वासुकिः।।२८।।

28. "I am Vajr among weapons, Kamdhenu among cows, Kamdev for procreation, and Vasuki, the king of snakes.

अनन्तश्चास्मि नागानां वरुणो यादसामहम्।
पितॄणामर्यमा चास्मि यमः संयमतामहम्।।२९।।

29. "I am Sheshnag among the nag (snakes), the god Varun among beings of water, Aryama among ancestors, and Yamraj among rulers."

प्रह्लादश्चास्मि दैत्यानां कालः कलयतामहम्।
मृगाणां च मृगेन्द्रोऽहं वैनतेयश्च पक्षिणाम्।।३०।।

30. "I am Prahlad among daitya (demons), unit of time for reckoners, the lion (mrigendr) among beasts, and Garud among birds."

पवनः पवतामस्मि रामः शस्त्रभृतामहम्।
झषाणां मकरश्चास्मि स्रोतसामस्मि जाह्नवी।।३१।।

31. "I am the wind among powers that refine, Ram among armed warriors, the crocodile among fishes, and the sacred Bhagirathi Ganga among rivers."

सर्गाणामादिरन्तश्च मध्यं चैवाहमर्जुन।
अध्यात्मविद्या विद्यानां वादः प्रवदतामहम्।।३२।।

32. "I am, O Arjun , the beginning and end and also the middle of created beings, the mystic knowledge of Self among sciences, and the final arbiter among disputants."

अक्षराणामकारोऽस्मि द्वन्द्वः सामासिकस्य च।
अहमेवाक्षयः कालो धाताहं विश्वतोमुखः।।३३।।

33. "I am the vowel akar among the letters of the alphabet, dwandwa among compounds, the eternal Mahakal amidst mutable time, and also the God who holds and sustains all."

मृत्युः सर्वहरश्चाहमुद्भवश्च भविष्यताम्।
कीर्तिः श्रीर्वाक्च नारीणां स्मृतिर्मेधा धृतिः क्षमा।।३४।।

34. "I am the death that annihilates all, the root of the creations to be, and Keerti among women-the embodiment of the feminine qualities of accomplishing action (keerti) vitality, speech, memory, awareness (medha), patience and forgiveness."

बृहत्साम तथा साम्नां गायत्री छन्दसामहम्।
मासानां मार्गशीर्षोऽहमृतूनां कुसुमाकरः।।३५।।

35. "And I am the Sam Ved among scriptural hymn, the Gayatri among metrical compositions, the ascendant Agrahayan among months, and the spring among seasons."

द्यूतं छलयतामस्मि तेजस्तेजस्विनामहम्।
जयोऽस्मि व्यवसायोऽस्मि सत्त्वं सत्त्ववतामहम्।।३६।।

36. "I am the deceit of cheating gamblers, the glory of renowned men, the victory of conquerors, the determination of the resolved, and the virtue of the pious."

वृष्णीनां वासुदेवोऽस्मि पाण्डवानां धनञ्जयः।
मुनीनामप्यहं व्यासः कवीनामुशना कविः।।३७।।

37. "I am Vasudev among the descendants of Vrishni, Dhananjay among the Pandav, Vedvyas among sages, and Shukracharya among poets."

दण्डो दमयतामस्मि नीतिरस्मि जिगीषताम्।
मौनं चैवास्मि गुह्यानां ज्ञानं ज्ञानवतामहम्।।३८।।

38. "And I am the oppression of tyrants, the wise conduct of those who aspire to succeed, silence among secrets, and also the knowledge of enlightened men."

यच्चापि सर्वभूतानां बीजं तदहमर्जुन।
न तदस्ति विना यत्स्यान्मया भूतं चराचरम्।।३९।।

39. "And, O Arjun, I am also the seed from which all beings have sprung up, because there is nothing animate or inanimate which is without my maya."

नान्तोऽस्ति मम दिव्यानां विभूतीनां परन्तप।
एष तूद्देशतः प्रोक्तो विभूतेर्विस्तरो मया।।४०।।

40. "What I have told you, O Parantap, is only a brief abstract of my countless glories."

यद्यद्विभूतिमत्सत्त्वं श्रीमदूर्जितमेव वा।
तत्तदेवावगच्छ त्वं मम तेजोंऽशसम्भवम्।।४१।।

41. "Know that whatever is possessed of glory, beauty, and strength has arisen from my own splendour."

अथवा बहुनैतेन किं ज्ञातेन तवार्जुन।
विष्टभ्याहमिदं कृत्स्नमेकांशेन स्थितो जगत्।।४२।।

42. "Or, instead of knowing anything more, O Arjun, just remember that I am here and I bear the whole world with just a fraction of my power."

Pauri 36

Gian Khand Mahin Gyan Prachand

Tithe Naad Binod Kaud Anand

Saram Khand Ki Bani Roop

Tithe Gharat Ghariye Bahut Anup

Ta Kian Gallan Kathian Na Jahi

Je Ko Kahe Pichhey Pachhutai

Tithe Ghariye Surti Mati Man Buddh

Tithe Ghariye Suran Siddhan Ki Sudh

Explanation

In this Pauri the importance of the expansion/increase of supreme divine knowledge leading towards the expanded wisdom of an individual is manifested. In the prolonged domain of divine knowledge, the knowledge is transformed into the divine enlightenment. Wisdom stage of divinity in a devotee as progresses, is converted/transformed into the stage of illumination of divine knowledge, which finally is merged into the God's Self –realization. Divine knowledge gets reflected in all activities of a devotee including his thoughts, words and performed activities. He just is unable to do or take up any other activity except that of divine/spiritual activity. This is the transformed stage after religious way of living and making substantial progress in accomplishing as well as crossing the stage of divine knowledge. In this stage of divine enlightenment, devotee enjoys blessing and grace of Almighty with complete intrinsic joy. In his deep mental state he experiences the primordial sound played by the heavenly melodies. This joy is beyond expression. He finds himself merged in intrinsic divine beauty, play, and melodies and in miraculous divine wonders.

After this realm of knowledge and divine enlightenment, realm of endeavor commences, which transforms the mind and makes it more and more beautiful with divine virtues/ qualities gradually. It means that the attribute of the divine knowledge is to make the intentions and deep rooted thinking of mind more refined and full of incomparable divine qualities. The inner meaning of this is to be conceived as follows: the religious life transform the soil; knowledge adds divine water to make it soft; to use it for giving the desired shape and form by the developed divine wisdom and beauty of the mind. Thus by the development of this state of endeavor, beauty appears in the mental frame and then only the exquisite forms are shaped. The developed purity and beauty in the mind contemplates in divine prospective, brings silence to its realm, which generates different varieties of arts, melodies, literature, scientific discoveries and divine manifestation to merge deeper in this beauty by intuition by the presence of Almighty. These happenings cannot be depicted. One, who tries to open up these mysteries of life of this higher evolution, finally ends up in repenting in the long run. This is because of the fact that such experience is always limited and it is never stable, and every moment fresh experience appears, which reopens a new fresh experience. This transforms the life gradually, which gives new shape with the storage of wonderful ever changing new experiences and thus transforming the state of mind that takes him to higher and higher realms. These all develop forged intuition, intellect, mind and deeper insight, which is beyond comprehension of a common human mind. The end results of manifestation of these inner qualities are to develop the devotee to the level of angels and seers having supernatural vision beyond the inception of a common human being.

In the nutshell, gradually development in spirituality brings the aspirant to the highest level of evolution to merge him in the glory of Almighty and liberate him from the cycles of births and death with the development and inception of supernatural qualities beyond the perception of a common human being.

Equivalent Verses of Srimad Bhagavad Gita (Pauri 36)

Chapter 9

The Royal Knowledge, The Royal Mystery

Direct Perception of God, Through Methods of Yoga "Easy to Perform" (Verses 1-3)

इदं तु ते गुह्यतमं प्रवक्ष्याम्यनसूयवे ।
ज्ञानं विज्ञानसहितं यज्ज्ञात्वा मोक्ष्यसेऽशुभात् ॥१॥

1. "The Lord said, 'I shall instruct you well with analogy in this mysterious knowledge, O the sinless, after knowing which you will be liberated from this sorrowful world.' "

राजविद्या राजगुह्यं पवित्रमिदमुत्तमम् ।
प्रत्यक्षावगमं धर्म्यं सुसुखं कर्तुमव्ययम् ॥२॥

2. "This (knowledge) is the monarch of all learning as well as of all mysteries, most sacred, doubtlessly propitious, easy to practise, and indestructible."

अश्रद्दधानाः पुरुषा धर्मस्यास्य परन्तप ।
अप्राप्य मां निवर्तन्ते मृत्युसंसारवर्त्मनि ॥३॥

3. "Men who have no faith in this knowledge, O Parantap, do not attain to me and are doomed to roaming about the mortal world."

Pauri - 37

Karam Khand Ki Bani Jore

Tithe Hore Na Koyee Hore

Tithe Jodh Mahabal Soor

Tin Mahin Ram Rahia Bharpoor

Tithe Sito Sita Mahima Mahin

Ta Ke Roop Na Kathane Jahin

Na Oh Maren Na Thage Jahin

Jin Ke Ram Vasen Man Mahin

Tithe Bhagat Vase Ke Loye

Karahin Anand Sacha Man Soye

Sach Khand Vase Nirankaar

Kar Kari Vekhe Nadar Nihal

Tithe Khand Mandal Varbhand

Je Ko Kathe Ta Ant Na Ant

Tithe Loye Loye Akaar

Jiv Jiv Hukam Tiven Tiv Kaar

Vekhe Vigse Kar Vichaar

Nanak Kathna Karra Saar

Explanation

As explained in the previous Pauris, after leading the religious life for a long time, spiritual aspirant enters in the new era of life, where he concentrates on various aspects of divine knowledge. When he cultivates gradually the assets of divine wisdom, he enters in the divine gate of religious austerities, the Sadhana, to get the glimpses of God's – realization. In this Pauri, it is made evident that without the blessings and grace of Almighty, one cannot climb the ladder of divinity any more with his own efforts. At this stage spiritual aspirant starts realizing this mysterious aspect in the path of divinity. He feels helpless and experiences the stage of effortlessness to make any further progress. He fully visualizes that ·in the realm of God's grace only the spiritual power prevails. Except His grace on the devotee, there is nothing else that can avail and show/direct him to the path of enlightenment. Integration, the union with Almighty is only feasible by His grace. His grace is as per His Wish and command. No power in the Universe can force Him. Only by His grace devotee is merged in His glory. By his own efforts, wish and desire, devotee cannot achieve any more in the path of Self-realization. Had it been possible then the path to Almighty becomes easy, and comes in the hands of a devotee and not in the command of Almighty. God is infinite, devotee being finite, on arriving at the doorsteps of His grace; he has to pray for His grace only. His Wish is the ultimate and final. When devotee is bestowed the grace of Almighty then all vices disappear. Only purity of mind prevails near the divine fire of His grace, no ill tendencies and vices can stay. Only Almighty and His beloved devotee exist in that higher ·stage of His regime. In other words, blessings of Almighty are supreme, all powerful, vices burn in divine fire and only perfect purity prevails in all respects of thoughts, words and deeds. In this highest state of the devotees, being in the realm of Almighty, only powerful warriors and heroes like Ram, the Almighty, inscribed in their hearts, could exist and thus, they enjoy the divine glory. They experience the presence of the grace of Almighty in each and every cell of their body and mind, and nothing beyond this prevails.

All those, who are blessed with divine grace and immerged in the glory of Almighty, their hearts are wedded and completely integrated with the divine greatness as the thread in garland is immerged in the fragrance of the flowers it is in contact with. The thread is glorified in the same way as the flowers. The thread gets the opportunity to be near to the god/goddess, where the garland is offered. There is no difference in the placement of flowers and the thread joining the flowers. In fact the thread last longer than the flowers. In the same way devotees is honored with more glory getting merged in divinity and becoming one with the divine glory. The devotee under this stage of mergence is blessed with exquisite graces, which are difficult to define. Their faces shine and enlightened with divine grace. In whose heart, the God, the Ram, the Almighty resides, they neither die and nor are enticed. Such devotees become liberated in this birth even having the physical body. They are always in the divine grace as and when they wish. However, they live in this delusive world but they are not affected by the tricks of delusion. They become self -realized souls. They are always in divine joy along with many more devotees from all over the universe. The society of self-realized devotees is class-less. Any one who achieves that higher state of realization from any source, from any cult, always find himself in the state of joy. This is because of the universal fact that God is omnipotent, omniscient, true, change-less, beyond time and is present in His true form in all His creatures giving them joy when they achieve that highest state and become one with all. All worship the same cosmic power and realize the same in the depth of their hearts. In fact devotees from all regions congregate there, rapt in the bliss of Almighty being perfectly pure from their hearts.

After this the devotee enters the highest state, the realm of truth, the changeless, the timeless state. In this realm of truth, he finds, he experiences the formless God, the omnipresent force. In this state, the concentrated power of Almighty is experienced, however he experiences the same power in all other states of evolution but in scattered and some what diluted form. In this realm of truth, devotee experiences the formless powerful form of Almighty, watching His universal creation with bounteous grace. In other words, the source of Almighty power originates from this location/state and is spread continuously all round like the sunlight, and thus He takes care of His creation and monitors the creation. This state of Almighty, the realm of truth is so mysterious and wonderful that there devotee finds existence of countless orbs, regions and origin of different firmaments. To have such an account is beyond description. In this state of existence, Almighty is not different from the devotee. Devotee and God merge in each other, both are in unison. Awareness of a devotee disappears. The awareness of the devotee and the Lord become the same. In this state of unison, it looks Almighty is everywhere and the devotees become the inseparable part of His existence. Nothing can be described in this state of existence as if devotees after mergence in Him are everywhere.

There are countless forms and worlds beyond worlds. All are functioning as per His ordains. At this highest stage of realization, it becomes very evident to a devotee that every act of this universe is as per His command. He experiences all this very closely without any doubt. A devotee realizes that Almighty clearly observes, watches, beholds every situation, He contemplates, enjoys and takes utmost care of His creation as per His set norms. It is all much harder than steel to express and relate functioning of His ways to manage the universe. After merging completely in the glory of Almighty, all these functioning as per His Wish are experienced but cannot be expressed by any mode. Guru Nanak Ji says that this is the experience of the devotee merged in unison with God and similarly the expression of the Lord managing the entire Cosmos. In short, this is the expression of God and that of the devotee totally merged in that highest state of formless Almighty.

Equivalent Verses of Srimad Bhagavad Gita (Pauri 37)

Chapter 12

Bhagti Yoga, Union Through Devotion

Should the Yogi Worship the Unmanifest, or a Personal God? (Verses 5-7)

क्लेशोऽधिकतरस्तेषामव्यक्तासक्तचेतसाम् ।
अव्यक्ता हि गतिर्दुःखं देहवद्भिरवाप्यते ।।५।।

5. "Achievement of perfection by men who are devoted to
the formless God is more arduous, because they who feel
conceited because of their physical bodies find it more
difficult to realize the unmanifest."

ये तु सर्वाणि कर्माणि मयि सन्यस्य मत्पराः ।
अनन्येनैव योगेन मां ध्यायन्त उपासते ।।६।।
तेषामहं समुद्धर्ता मृत्युसंसारसागरात् ।
भवामि नचिरात्पार्थ मय्यावेशितचेतसाम् ।।७।।

6-7. "And, O Parth, I soon deliver my affectionate devotees
who have set their mind on me and who, coming under my
shelter and dedicating all their action to me, ever
contemplate and worship me-the manifest God-with
unshaken intentness, from the abyss of the mortal world."

Pauri -38

Explanation

In this Pauri divine virtues are listed and means to cultivate these virtues are expressed. It is expressed that to climb the ladder to achieve the God's realization, number of obstacles come on the path that tend to stop a devotee towards the further movement to progress. It is advised that self-restraint, the continence, to be made/considered as furnace to burn various vices to make the divine path smooth and steady. In other words one must control his senses for the undue worldly pleasures by all possible means. Continence conserves energy and this preserved energy can be concentrated to achieve the desired aim of life of self-realization. Continence has power to create wonders by the grace of Almighty to allow the flow of energy in the required channels. Without strengthening the continence, one cannot make any significance progress in any direction. Another significant quality is the cultivation of patience. Patience of the mind must act as goldsmith of this shop of mental frame to forge the trend of life in various complex situations. One must try to tackle every situation of life with utmost patience. Patience must be made the governing factor to act and decide. Divine supreme knowledge, which has been cultivated with time in climbing the ladder of spirituality and through the divine religious books of Vedas, to be made weapons to sharpen the existing wisdom to decide the appropriate path to be followed in the course of life to achieve the self-realization and to tackle the complex issues. At time the sharp wisdom, intuition, silence of mind and blessings of the Almighty can only come for rescue and also to show the enlightened path of realization.

The fear of God in the mind background must be the bellow to strengthen the intensity of fire to increase its temperature to burn the sins and various vices of the mind easily and faster to lead a pure and divine life so as to concentrate on the goal of mergence in the glory of the Lord. The fear gives sunburn concentration, and does not allow the mind to wander. Fear for positive gain, showers strength to the mind. Fear for selfish motives to harm others only shatters the mind and invite nervousness. The fear of God, who is omnipresent, can maintain the penance of self-restrain in the hearts of devotees to keep away from worldly vices. When mind becomes completely pure and chaste in all respects then only nectar of divine love will be generated in its deep roots by the grace of Almighty. Divinity will appear in the form of His name/japa and grace in the heart of the devotees. The pot of the heart will be filled with love of the God. Then only the truth will emerge from the true mint. This true mint will produce by itself the divine words, which are divine virtues and are governed by self restrain/continence, patience, divine wisdom/ knowledge, divine experience, fear of Lord, penance, divine love and God's name/glory. These eight qualities are the core source of divine truth and these are the true mint that generate the divine words, which acts as gate way, the doors of entry to the divine home to merge with the Almighty and become one with Him. These are the eight means, which Guru Nanak Ji has expressed to show the path of mergence with divine light.

Here the mystery of God's realization is expressed that says by means this eight fold means, divine words appear and these words become the guiding force that can take the devotees to the door-steps of self-realization. However, this is feasible by the grace and the mercy of God. Those devotees are really blessed whom divine grace is bestowed. Guru Nanak Ji says that Almighty by His merciful glance blesses all such devotees and directs them towards the right path of mergence in Him.

Equivalent Verses of Srimad Bhagavad Gita (Pauri 38)

Chapter 12

Bhagti Yoga: Union Through Devotion

Qualities of the Devotee, Endearing to God (Verses 13-20)

अद्वेष्टा सर्वभूतानां मैत्रः करुण एव च।
निर्ममो निरहङ्कारः समदुःखसुखः क्षमी।।१३।।
सन्तुष्टः सततं योगी यतात्मा दृढनिश्चयः।
मय्यर्पितमनोबुद्धिर्यो मद्भक्तः स मे प्रियः।।१४।।

13-14. "The devotee who has malice towards none and loves all, who is compassionate and free from attachment and vanity, who views sorrow and joy equally and is forgiving, endowed with steady yog, contented alike with both profit and loss, restrained in mind, and dedicated to me with firm conviction, is dear to me."

यस्मान्नोद्विजते लोको लोकान्नोद्विजते च यः।
हर्षामर्षभयोद्वेगैर्मुक्तो यः स च मे प्रियः।।१५।।

15. "The devotee who does not upset anyone, nor is upset by anyone, and who is free from the contradictions of joy, envy, and fear, is dear to me."

अनपेक्षः शुचिर्दक्ष उदासीनो गतव्यथः।
सर्वारम्भपरित्यागी यो मद्भक्तः स मे प्रियः।।१६।।

16. "The devotee who is emancipated from desire, pure, dexterous at his task, impartial, free from sorrow, and who has achieved the state of actionlessness, is dear to me."

यो न हृष्यति न द्वेष्टि न शोचति न काङ्क्षति।
शुभाशुभपरित्यागी भक्तिमान्यः स मे प्रियः ।।१७।।

17. "The devotee who is neither joyous nor envious, neither troubled nor concerned, and who has given up all good and evil actions, is dear to me."

समः शत्रौ च मित्रे च तथा मानापमानयोः।
शीतोष्णसुखदुःखेषु समः सङ्गविवर्जितः।।१८।।
तुल्यनिन्दास्तुतिर्मौनी सन्तुष्टो येन केनचित्।
अनिकेतः स्थिरमतिर्भक्तिमान्मे प्रियो नरः।।१९।।

18-19. "The steady worshipper, who regards friends and foes, honour and dishonour, cold and heat, happiness and sorrow, as equal, and who is detached from the world, indifferent to slander and praise, meditative, contented with any manner of physical sustenance, and free from infatuation for the place where he dwells, is dear to me.

ये तु धर्म्यामृतमिदं यथोक्तं पर्युपासते।
श्रद्दधाना मत्परमा भक्तास्तेऽतीव मे प्रियाः।।२०।।

20. "And the devotees who rest in me and taste well the aforesaid nectar of dharm in a spirit of selflessness are the dearest to me."

Sloka - The Epilogue

Explanation

In this epilogue, Guru Nanak Ji has expressed the philosophy of existence in very simple and impressive words. In simple straight words it is said that air is Guru, water is father and earth is the great mother. The day and nights are nurses in whose lap the world plays. The mysterious and deeper meaning of this Sloka is quite difficult to express. However, it can be said that without food, one can live for a few days, without water for couple of hours but without air one cannot live even for a microsecond. Without breath, there is no life. Breathing process goes on automatically where as one need to consume food and drink water by self-efforts. So air, which a creature consumes constantly, is the master, the Guru, and without the guidance and direction of Guru, the light, the existence ceases. So, the air is regarded as Guru. Furthermore, air is woven with the Prana, the life force, which is the sole part of existence. A human being is declared dead when life force leaves a physical body. Life force is the instrument for functioning of all the vital elements of the system for movement of the cycle of life. So, the air is called the Guru, which is the gateway to the Almighty. If one can experience the life force mentally in his physical body and can monitor it by the grace of God, he can climb the ladder of self-realization by the blessings of Almighty. This is basic prerequisite of spiritual development. That is the reason air is Guru and by its assistance one can merge in Almighty and realizes Him.

Water is like the father since one third of universe is water and our body has one-third by volume water only. Water transmits coolness and cleans, maintains our system. Most of human works/activities go around water only. There is no life without water. Water is the nucleus of human life for all his activities. Without father there is no creation and so without water, there is no existence/life. Mother earth acts like mother in our life. She grows food to feeds us. Take care of our excreta, dissolve in her and maintains her beauty and her surroundings. Mother is supreme in all respects to get our life moving smoothly. One gets education from mother, father and Guru. The fellow is blessed if he gets supreme mother, father and master, so that he gets proper virtues and wisdom and the supreme knowledge of God's realization.

Furthermore, air cannot be controlled in the boundaries. It is formless like Almighty; it is like cosmic light that guides the human being. It is supernal, the guide to our soul. Water is like mind in a human being. It can go any where by changing its form. It is forceful entity. Earth mother is like physical body and takes care of basic physical needs. In fact, body is mother earth, water is mind and soul is the air .All physical being have body, human being have mind of various levels of development and only spiritually evolved have evolved soul that can merge in air/the Pranic light, the supernal. The play of day and night in this universe is for our safety, joy and nourishment. Day and night are the representative of the time, and by their presence this worldly play is going on by the process of relishing the energy and using it as needed.

In the span of lifetime, human being does all type of actions. Out of all his actions, some of them are good and some actions are not good, not healthier, may be sinful, might be executed intentionally or might have been done unintentionally. The lord of justices' watches all good and bad deeds. Every action is judged based on its merit. If one is pure, he will be near to God. One can execute no sinful action if he is nearer to the God. If the actions executed by some one are not good, and are sinful, it indicates that Almighty does not bless him. Divine virtues are far away from him. In other words some action draw closeness to Him and other action shall further recede him from Almighty. However, God is stable under all conditions. Only individual actions change his location with respect to Almighty. What one reaps that he gets. All fruits to an individual are the resultant of his right and wrong actions. So, one need not to blame others for troubles and miseries of own life. One himself is responsible for all his troubles. This must be very clearly understood and well conceived. Almighty is like fire. Whosoever is near to the him, get his warmth, and it holds good by the Almighty. More one is closer to Almighty; he is showered more of His blessings. But at the same time Almighty is kind to His devotees, likes and favors the lovable devotees and also, He is the perfect judge for them

Those, who merge in the glory of Almighty, mediate on Him; He dissolves all miseries of such devotional devotees. Such devotees are perfect in their austerities. In fact such devotees don't have any desire and they don't demand any thing from Almighty. They are desire-less and all their activities are selfless. All miseries of life, they consider the divine gift from Almighty. Those who are merged in His glory, their faces are graceful, their actions their company, their deeds are praise worthy. Even company of such people liberates the fellow being.

In general, those who meditate are able to sublimate their toil. Guru Nanak Ji says, such people have effulgent bright faces, and they are able to redeem many others with their strides.

Equivalent Verses Of Srimad Bhagavad Gita (Sloka - The Epilogue)

Chapter 9

The Royal Knowledge, The Royal Mystery

The Right Method of worshiping God (Verses 27-34)

यत्करोषि यदश्नासि यज्जुहोषि ददासि यत् ।
यत्तपस्यसि कौन्तेय तत्कुरुष्व मदर्पणम् ।।२७।।

27. "You should, O son of Kunti, dedicate to me whatever you do, eat, offer as sacrifice, give as alms, and also your penance."

शुभाशुभफलैरेवं मोक्ष्यसे कर्मबन्धनैः ।
सन्न्यासयोगयुक्तात्मा विमुक्तो मामुपैष्यसि ।।२८।।

28. "Possessed thus of the yog of renunciation by the sacrifice of all your acts, you will be freed from good as well as evil fruits which are the shackles of action, and attain to me."

समोऽहं सर्वभूतेषु न मे द्वेष्योऽस्ति न प्रियः ।
ये भजन्ति तु मां भक्त्या मयि ते तेषु चाप्यहम् ।।२९।।

29. "Although I abide evenly in all beings and there is no one who is either dear or hateful to me, worshippers who contemplate me with loving devotion abide in me and I in them."

अपि चेत्सुदुराचारो भजते मामनन्यभाक् ।
साधुरेव स मन्तव्यः सम्यग्व्यवसितो हि सः ।।३०।।

30. "Even if a man of the most depraved conduct worships me incessantly, he is worthy of being regarded as a saint because he is a man of true resolve."

क्षिप्रं भवति धर्मात्मा शश्वच्छान्तिं निगच्छति।
कौन्तेय प्रति जानीहि न मे भक्तः प्रणश्यति।।३१।।

31. "Thus he shortly grows pious and achieves eternal peace, and so, O son of Kunti, you Should know beyond any doubt that my worshipper is never destroyed."

मां हि पार्थ व्यपाश्रित्य येऽपि स्युः पापयोनयः।
स्त्रियो वैश्यास्तथा शूद्रास्तेऽपि यान्ति परां गतिम्।।३२।।

32. "Since even women, Vaishya and Shudr, whose births are regarded as inferior , attain, O Parth, to the supreme goal by taking refuge in me..."

किं पुनर्ब्राह्मणाः पुण्या भक्ता राजर्षयस्तथा।
अनित्यमसुखं लोकमिमं प्राप्य भजस्व माम्।।३३।।

33. "It hardly needs saying that since pious Brahmin and royal sages (rajarshi) attain to salvation, you should also renounce this miserable, ephemeral, mortal body and always engage in my worship."

मन्मना भव मद्भक्तो मद्याजी मां नमस्कुरु।
मामेवैष्यसि युक्त्वैवमात्मानं मत्परायणः।।३४।।

34. "If, taking refuge in and with a total devotion of the Self to me, you contemplate, remember with humble reverence, and worship only me (Vasudev), you will attain to me."